T0209492

About the Book

"If inner peace and a sense of justice come only from God (Proverbs 29:26; Shadrach et al. vs. Nebuchadnezzar, Daniel 3) and we yearn for both when in conflict, why do we not appropriate them from God when in conflict? I John, 4:18 suggests it is because we stand paralyzed in fear, for our love is not fully mature. But how can that be true for a forgiven Believer—unless our image of God is not correct?

"The author argues that our fear flows from an image of God as an angry judge, judging us from his Torah, a penal code of crime and punishment. But why do we think that when Christ on the cross wipes our sins away and gives us a spirit of sonship? (Romans 8:15). Do we think it because we think our thousand-year Western legal tradition is biblically based and we subconsciously read it into Torah? What if that premise is wrong? After all, Torah originally meant instructions or teachings, not law.

"Mr. Bontrager reexamines the nature of God and his Word in view of Torah as a gracious gift of instructions to people blinded by sin, living in a fallen world, offered to us by God to guide us in working through conflict according to his Ways, thereby finding peace and justice (Psalm 119)."

SEEKING PEACE & JUSTICE

Your Image of God Matters

William Bontrager J.D.

William "Bill" Bontrager, J.D.
4765 East 25th St., Tucson, AZ 85711
H - (520) 638-6676; C - (520) 638-6504
wdb@ftitel.net; www.shepherdsforpeace.com

WESTBOW
PRESS®
A DIVISION OF THOMAS NELSON
& ZONDERVAN

WestBow Press books may be ordered through booksellers or by contacting:

WestBow Press
A Division of Thomas Nelson & Zondervan
1663 Liberty Drive
Bloomington, IN 47403
www.westbowpress.com
1 (866) 928-1240

ISBN: 978-1-9736-5221-2 (sc)
ISBN: 978-1-9736-5220-5 (e)

Print information available on the last page.

WestBow Press rev. date: 02/08/2019

Contents

Citations

Except as noted, all quotations of law-terms are from *Black's Law Dictionary, 10ᵗʰ Ed.*, (Bryan A Gardner; 2014). Used with permission of Thomson-West Publishers, www.Thomsonreuters.com ISBN #9780314613004.

All translations of Hebrew and Geek words are taken from *Vine's Expository Dictionary of Biblical Words*, by W.E. Vine, M.A., Merrill F. Unger, Th.M., Th.D., Ph.D., and William White, Jr., Th.M, Ph.D. authors; Copyright 1985 by Thomas Nelson, Inc., Publishers. Used by permission of Thomas Nelson. www.thomasnelson.com<https://thomasnelson.com/>

All quotations from the Bible are from *The Amplified Topical Reference Bible*, Copyright 1987, used by permission of The Zondervan Corporation and Lockman Foundation, Library of Congress Card #2005934717.

Quotation from pg xi from *Instruments In The Redeemer's Hands: People in Need of Change Helping People in Need of Change*, by Paul David Tripp, (2002), ISBN #978-0-87552-607-2 used by permission of P&R Publishing Co., P.O. Box 817, Phillipsburgh, N.J., www.prpbooks.com

Quotation from pgs 4-6, *The Institutes of Biblical Law*, by Rousas John Rushdoony (1973), ISBN #978-0-87552-410-8, used by permission from P&R Publishing Co., P.O. Box 817, Phillipsburgh N.J., 08865, www.prpbooks.com

Quotations from pgs 1 and 51-53, *A theology of Christian Counseling: More Than Redemption*, by Jay E. Adams (1979) ISBN #0-310-51101-1 used by permission from Nouthetic.org

Quotations from pgs iii, 4, 6, *The Nature and Functions of Law*, by Harold J. Berman, © The Foundation Press, Inc., (1958) used by permission of West Academic, westacademic.com

Dedication

To Ellen, my wife of 57 years, who has stuck with me through thick to thin.

To Peter, Matt, Laury, Charlie, Sam, Tim, Ken, and the rest of the early CCS'ers for their trail blazing, comradeship and challenges.

To Chuck Colson for vision, financial support, and encouragement.

To Danny, Daryl, Margaret and the gang at ICCS for taking in and sending forth a non-PhD.

To Vaghan, Dunayev, and Erigep for opening their hearts and hospitality to us, and for constant protection while in their lands.

To the One Who made us all, for His salvation, faithfulness, goodness, and provision.

Prologue

It's February 1st, 1994. I am 53 years old, and my wife, Ellen, and I are 30,000 feet up in the air and headed into Moscow — Russia, not Idaho – with 10-70 pound boxes in the hold, and four carry-ons.

There had been a phone call from a Russian lawyer to a U.S. lawyer asking for someone to come to Moscow State Open University to:

> "Teach us the meaning of the Western Words of Law and
> their moral foundation, for we know better than most that
> law without a moral foundation is worthless."

The U.S. lawyer called the International Institute for Christian Studies (IICS; now Global Scholars) in Kansas, and passed the word on.

Daryl McCarthy of IICS had come to know Chuck Colson, and called Chuck to see if he might know of someone. Chuck said: "Try Bill Bontrager. He's now in Poland for me as a delegate to the U.N.'s Second International Conference on the Future of Corrections, but lives in Colorado and would likely jump at the chance." So Daryl wrote me.

Ellen, thinking it was a solicitation for money, threw it in the trash. A couple of days later, she dug it out and left it for me (unopened) for when I got back from Poland and Estonia. It was mid-October, 1993.

After interviewing with the folks at IICS in early November (I would be their first non-earned PhD to be sent out), it was a "go".

At that moment, I had been out of law for over 10-years.

To get ready to teach, and create at least two courses, I had to refresh myself on legal principles. I called a law school classmate, George Gossman who was with West Publishing, to see if I could beg some books for study and to take as an initial library for the University. George sent me a number of West' *Nutshells* on different legal subjects, and a bunch of other books for the library. [3, 70-pound boxes! CD's of law books did not yet exist.]

As I started reading, I was reading with a background of:

a) son of a judge, prosecutor, legislator father;
b) raised in the Presbyterian Church of my "full of grace and mercy" mother
c) Believer in God seeking after an understanding of justice;
d) 1966 Indiana University Law School grad; J.D. degree;
e) general practice of law 1966-1976, Elkhart, Indiana;
f) Chairman of the Indiana Board of Correction, a lay- citizen advisory board to the Governor of Indiana on prisons, 1974-1976;
g) Judge (disgraced), Elkhart Superior Court II, 1/1/77- 2/14/82 [see: Colson, *Loving God*, Chpt. 16, Zondervan, 1983];
h) a childhood understanding that the most fundamental principles of our Western Law and Legal Systems were Biblically based; and,
i) 10-years out of law while in a Reconciliation Ministry helping Christians in conflict.

So here I am, buckled in at 30,000', and wondering why the principles of law I am reading in the *Nutshells* are so obviously not Biblical, and don't match up with God's purpose for law and His method for dealing with conflict which I have spent 10-years studying in the Old & New Testaments!

What am I going to do? I can't teach moral foundations of our Western Law which are not Godly — unless, unless — can I do it by a critique against God's way for us to deal with conflict and get away with it in a totalitarian system?

But what if all my thoughts and feelings are crazy?

Well, I have to tighten the belt; we are headed down and there is a blizzard at Sheremetyevo II airport. Vaghan is to be there and meet us and our 10 boxes. Like it or not, here we go!

How does a person with my background end up crossing a bridge over the Moskva River at 2:00am, with four 70-lb boxes on top of a very small car, 5 more boxes and 4 carry-ons inside, two people plus Yevgeny driving (who speaks no English and we speak no Russian) — and just what is it I think I have discovered about God, His *torah*, and *Justice*?

Oh, one box got lost, which is why there were 9 and not 10, if you are counting and wondering.

Foreword

If possible, as far as it depends on you,
live at peace with everyone.
Roms. 12:18.

Many crave *and* seek the ruler's favor,
but the wise man [waits] for justice from the Lord.
Prov. 29:26

Salom OT:7965 — peace; completeness; welfare; health.
Mah slomka OT: – "What is your peace," "how are you doing."
Vine's, Greek pgs 173-174

Chapter 12 of Romans might easily be considered the start of the second of two points in a lawyer's Brief entitled:

"How fallen people, saved by God and in indwelt with the Holy Spirit, can live at peace in a fallen world surrounded by fallen people."

The first 11 chapters had covered the matter of "Who was, is, and will be Jesus Christ, and who are you in Christ?"

Paul was, of course, a lawyer, Pharisee of Pharisees. [Philippians. 3:4-6; Acts 22:3.]

But it is important to note that Paul was not merely a lawyer; he was a *litigating lawyer*, a *Prosecutor* of Believers for violation of the black-letter "Law of The Lord" (God's *Torah*).

At least that is what he was when he encountered the God whom he thought he knew and understood but did not understand while on the road to Damascus. [Acts 9:1-8.]

What Paul came to see was that his image of God, based upon his understanding of the Old Testament Scriptures as given him by the Jewish society in which he was raised, was full of errors. Once his image of God changed, Paul went on to be the primary author of the New Testament.

But why was Paul's image faulty to begin with?

I posit that Paul's image was faulty because God's *Torah* had been twisted from *Good Instructions* from God conveyed directly to the people at the foot of the Mountain before all but Moses withdrew in terror [see Exodus 20:18-21] into "Law" over the course of 1800-years prior to Jesus.

A whole culture had grown up around the meaning of *Torah* as "Law" which insinuated itself into a reading of the Scriptures as a penal code. That understanding had become "Holy Writ," to the point that it could not be challenged without being crucified.

Until, that is, Paul reconsidered it all in light of God personified in the flesh of Jesus.

I write today to people who:

a) call Jesus of Nazareth their Lord and Savior,
b) are 2000 years after His death, burial and Resurrection,
c) have been raised in a cultural lens of a Western Legal Philosophy which has, from my research and life experiences, insinuated itself into the Bible, and,
d) while being familiar with the Bible and the pulpit presentation of Jesus the Christ and the Bible as black-letter Law,
e) do not know or comprehend the truth of the One Who created them and rescues them though faith in Christ.

I believe that our belief that the fundamental principles of our Western Law are Biblically based has twisted us as badly as Paul's society had twisted him — and our image of God, like Paul's image of God, is not a *proper* image of the God whom we proclaim and desire to serve.

I write to ask the Reader: "Is your image of God faulty?"

I write because mine was faulty for the first 53-years of my life, and likely still incomplete in many respects.

I write because the Reader will never be able to "live at peace", or sleep in the peace of the *just* while on this earth, unless his/her image of God is a *proper* image, and they are walking His path. Otherwise, fear will impede them from practicing His ways for finding peace and justice in the midst of a conflict [I John 4:18].

So let us start by being truthful with one another: A very large portion of our lives involves conflict — with self, God and others — and we are not likely to have peace or justice unless we deal with those conflicts according to God's ways rather than man's ways.

But to come to be willing to risk trying His way, we have to truly know and understand God and His Word devoid of the philosophies of our Western Legal Tradition.

I also write because my models for peace when in conflict are Adam and Eve [Gen. 3], and Shadrach, Meshach, and Abednego [Daniel 3]. They found it. I have often found it. And you can find it if you are willing to consider the possibility that your image of God is wrong.

The Change in Paul — and in Me

After his "road trip", Paul disappeared into the wilderness, where he spent several years reviewing all the Old Testament Scriptures in light of the image of God which he saw in Christ when he met Him on the road to Damascus — and also saw Him in the form of Ananias, whom he had come to persecute and who now stood quaking while hugging the blinders off of Paul!

I can just hear the Holy Spirit: "Paul, do you think you are crazy? Do you think this theology can't work? Look at who's hugging you!"

During his time in the wilderness Paul was away from community influence, and the teaching of any of its distortions. At the end of his study, Paul chose to throw away his prior theology, and installed a new theology in his mind and heart. I suggest he was able to do this because his image of God had changed.

I, like Paul, was a litigating lawyer, Presbyterian in Bible thought, living at a time when family, church, school and society all proclaimed that the fundamental philosophies of our Criminal Code and Legal Systems are Biblically based.

I have been an advisor to governments on matters of crime and punishment, and a trial court judge. [Full disclosure: if you dig around in the Web, you will find that I am, to the world, a disgraced former judge and disgraced former lawyer; stories for another day. But I am at peace over those things.]

It was while serving as a judge that I both saw myself as a sinner- of-nature in need a Savior, and of my need to not just accept God's free gift, but to surrender to Christ as my Lord for daily life.

In 1992-94, because of my journey in life away from the law, I began to question the idea that the philosophies behind our criminal laws and systems are Biblically based. After considerable study, prayer and counsel with fellow believers, I have chosen to reject that proposition.

And that has changed my image of God away from one of Him sitting high above, robed in black with law books to one side and a balance scales to the other, a sword laying flat on the bench before Him, and a long arm with a bony finger pointed directly at me.

We know what Paul's theology was before confrontation with Christ. It was: "Obey the Law of the Lord and you will be saved from the wrath of God. And if you argue a contrary nature of God, I will be happy in my righteousness to slay you."

After his confrontation on the road, Paul's theology became (my paraphrase):

> We are sinners of nature, unable to stand in the presence of God, and doomed to death for our sins.
>
> But God has extended grace to all through the death, burial and resurrection of His only begotten Son, Jesus Christ of Nazareth, so that those who believe on that fact, in faith, and then choose to submit to Jesus as Lord of their lives, will be restored to right-relationship with God for eternity; i.e., their sins — past, present and future — would be forgiven and washed away in the acceptance of Jesus as God's sacrificial death for the death we all deserve.
>
> Additionally, God would graciously send His Holy Spirit to indwell those who believe, so they might walk with God along- side and assisting them as He did Adam and Eve in the Garden pre-Fall.
>
> In short, Man's works-philosophy of legalistic obedience to God's *Law* to secure salvation was abolished, and God's pre- Fall plan of Grace through Christ was implemented.

Now, my theology growing up was not dissimilar:

> (a) God is, was, and ever will be; (b) I would face Him someday to answer for my life; (c) He would be seated high, with white wig, pinch-nez glasses, black robe, law book, balance scale and sword; (d) He would declare my actions and inactions, placing them on His balance scale of right and wrong; **but**, (e) I would be allowed to make final argument over where He placed any given item and,

in comparison to others whom I knew or met or had heard of, I was a decent person and would pass His examination.

This is, of course, a pure "work's theology."

In the fall of 1977, while serving as Judge, I, like Paul, had an encounter with God "up close and personal," and was transformed.

I had been on the Bench for 9 months, and discovered that not only could I not do justice because of the black letter of the Law I was tasked to enforce, but was often, in my opinion, doing injustice.

I came to the conclusion that "We the People" could not "establish justice" as we had proclaimed in the preamble to the U.S. Constitution. [In fact, all of the promises of the Preamble can only be fulfilled by God, not man; but that is another item for another time.]

One Friday evening, with that construct of life and full of anger at the futility of it all, I boldly called God a fraud, and told Him to give the Aardvark a chance next time.

And then we had a "conversation" inside my mind:

> "It's okay, Judge; I know what is taking place, and have made provision for it." [His use of my title seemed strange to me; I've always been "just plain Bill" in my mind. But it was what I was at the time]

> "In a pig's eye! If so, why don't I see it?"

> "Well, Bill, you don't know you're a sinner." [The sudden personalization stunned me, and made me very uncomfortable.]

> "But I do", and rattled through my mind a list of my sins.

> "Bill, do you recall the man you sent to prison for life for the rape of a 2-year old? Do you recall how you felt, what you wanted to do to him, and where you would do it? [Oh yeah: high noon at the busiest intersection in town!] Well, I feel the same about you."

It was then that I realize that I was not a person who sinned and needed to work harder, but a "sinner in my essential character". As such a person, I needed a Savior, for my self- oriented works would never suffice.

Suddenly all I had learned about Jesus while growing up clicked into place — and so I accepted Jesus as God's Christ and my Savior.

However, I didn't have the luxury of going off alone for several years to rethink things — I had court on Monday!

In 1981, through a series of events, I came to see myself as strapped to a railroad track, with a train of the law coming downhill at me, with no one at the controls, and no way to get off the track. I was unable to control anything — and I suddenly realized I had never once asked the One I asked to save me what He would have me do.

And so I surrendered myself, family (without asking them for permission), job, license to practice law, and all we had, to Him Who saves — and I found peace in the midst of a maelstrom which was then swirling about me. [If you want to know more about the maelstrom, Chuck Colson wrote about it in chapter 16 of his book, *Loving God* [Zondervan, 1983]. The chapter title is *Contra Mundo*, i.e., "Against the World", but should have been, "A Fool's Foot In His Own Mouth".]

In 1982, I left the Bench, and in 1983 the law, and Elkhart.

Ellen and I, along and our two youngest, moved to Minneapolis to direct the Christian Conciliation Service [CCS] of Minnesota. For the next ten years, I was immersed in seeking to understand what God had to say about conflict and its sources, how God wants us to deal with it, how we are to offer help others who are in it, and where does the Body of Christ come into play in all of this.

By 1992, my theology had changed to that of the transformed Paul. But it left me with a question:

As a sinner living among sinners in a fallen world, where can I turn for wise counsel on how to live? I certainly can't trust my deceptively wicked heart and darkened mind.

My answer to my own question was, and remains:

> To: (a) God in prayer; (b) His Scriptures as *good and gracious instructions for life;* (c) the Body of Christ for wisdom and support; and (4) the Holy Spirit for counsel and moment by moment direction.

In Philippians 2:12-13, Paul's expressed the impact of his change in theology in the following way:

> Therefore, my dear ones, as you have always obeyed [my suggestions], so now, not only [with the enthusiasm you would show] in my presence but much more because I am absent, <u>work out</u> (cultivate, carry out to the goal, and fully complete) your own salvation <u>with reverence *and* awe</u> and trembling (self-distrust, with serious caution, tenderness of conscience, watchfulness against temptation, timidly shrinking from whatever might offend God and discredit the name of Christ). [Not in your own strength] for it is God Who is all the while effectually at work in you [energizing and creating in you the power and desire], both to will and to work for His good pleasure *and* satisfaction *and* delight.

Neither Paul's theology nor my theology are a Work's Theology, for both flow from the first part of Paul's Brief, i.e., who Christ was/is, who we are in Him and why, therefore, we follow Him out of love and not terror!

Paul's "Therefore" in Romans 12:1 incorporates all of chapters 1-11 into the second part of his Brief. In those first 11 chapters, Paul had explained God's *plan for man in the light of sin entering the world,* from the beginning of time. One Who would create such a plan can hardly be thought of as an angry judge waiting to destroy His creation.

Paul did not presume that his readers either knew or did not know the things about which he wrote, but he knew they needed to know, understand and experience those basics in their fullness in order to be able to practice the Ways of God and live at peace in a fallen world among fallen people.

So Paul laid the foundation, which I beg you to prayerfully re-read while contemplating your existing image of God.

What Paul went on to explain in the remainder of Romans is of no value whatsoever to anyone who: (a) does not understand the first 11 chapters; and, (b) does not have a proper image of God the Father.

Finally, in all that I am going to say about what I believe the Scriptures present about the Image of God, you should know that I have two principle ways of reading the Scriptures:

1. As God's gracious gift to a fallen Universe, designed to: (a) help us see and understand Him and ourselves; (b) as wise instruction and exhortation for how to live in a fallen Universe; and, (c) knowing that the Scripture are not a code of crime and punishment.

2. By constantly running every word of Scripture through the picture I have from Genesis 3, and God walking the world in His Son, Jesus of Nazareth, to see if the words are true to the model — and checking the Hebrew and Greek when I detect fingernails on the blackboard of my heart that something is amiss.

Revisiting My Purpose in Writing

I am saddened by the fact that too many Christians, from the highest to the lowest, do not practice God's Ways for dealing with conflict, but go to courts, secular counselors, medical professionals and the like as frequently as un-believers — or they try to stuff their conflicts deep down inside where:

> … [a] root of resentment (rancor, bitterness, or hatred) shoots forth and causes trouble *and* bitter torment, and the many become defiled by it. [Hebrews. 12:15.]

> Let all bitterness and indignation *and* wrath (passion, rage, bad temper) and resentment (anger, animosity) and quarreling (brawling, clamor, contention) and slander (evil-speaking, abusive or blasphemous language) together with all malice (spite, ill will, or baseness of any kind [reside]." [Ephesians 4:31; *see also* I Corinthians. 6:7-8, and Matthew 5:25-26].

My Purpose in writing is to show that God has given us *very good instructions* on how to deal with conflicts of life so that we might: (a) receive His *Justice* [Proverbs. 29:26]; (b) do His *Justice* [Micah 6:8]; and, (c) live at peace, *salom*, when in the midst of a conflict [Daniel 3].

My Method will include trying to show that our image of God is improper if we read his *torah* (the entire Bible) as a Criminal Penal Code containing our secular legal philosophies, instead of reading it as *a gracious gift of instruction* for living at peace to people blinded by sin.

The Secular Philosophy of
Our Law and Systems

The first step towards wisdom is to know some things about our law and its systems, so we can then compare and contrast them with what God says about conflict in the Bible.

The secular philosophy undergirding our criminal, allegedly "just" system, is a series of steps as follows:

1. Publish the Law, and <u>presume</u> all know it in its fullness — a false premise, for none (including judges and attorneys) can ever know it all in all of its complexity, particularly in this day and age.

2. Declare the punishment for the Law-breaker, and impose the punishment, for if we do not impose a punishment the system will fail to meet its *purpose*.

3. <u>Presume</u> that by punishing Person A for Crime X <u>we can deter all mankind</u> [a chief purpose of Law] from breaking <u>any</u> published Law as man, in his enlightened self-interest, will choose to obey the law rather than be punished; i.e., the Doctrine of *General Deterrence*, another false premise.

4. <u>Presume</u> the state of the mind of the law-breaker (its intent, recklessness or negligence) by declaring that the doing of the act discloses the intent, and thereby justify our punishing "them" as being different than "us" — while we all remain sinners against God who allows us to live.

In contrast, God allows us to suffer the natural consequences of our actions so that, as we can't figure out what is going on with our lives, we will seek out Him for understanding and how to walk forward.

Conflict Defined:

Peace flees from us when we are in conflict, yet *Peace* and *Justice* are the longings of our hearts when in conflict. So, what do I mean by, *conflict*?

When I talk about *conflict*, I mean any imaginable conflict: (a) internal with self or God, including illnesses, addictions, besetting sins, psychological/psychiatric turmoil; and/or (b) external with others, be it crime, tort, contract, domestic relations, commercial relations, family relations, neighbor, church, political, etc. Any actual list would be endless, and it is the rare day in which one or another type does not pop up to rob us of our peace.

Conflicts are Satan's playground for deceiving us and allowing fear to rule us.

But conflicts are also God's character building/equipping school.

The *Source* of our conflicts, the *Implications* of our conflicts, the *Helps of God* available to us when in conflict, and *God's path to walk* when in conflict are all sketched out in James 4:1-10:

> **Source:** 1. What leads to strife (discord and feuds) and how do conflicts (quarrels and fightings) originate among you? Do they not arise from your sensual desires that are ever warring in your bodily members? You are jealous and covet [what others have] and your desires go unfulfilled; [so] you become murderers. [To hate is to murder as far as your hearts are concerned.] You burn with envy and anger and are not able to obtain [the gratification, the contentment, and the happiness that you seek], so you fight and war. You do not have, because you do not ask. [Or] you do ask [God for them] and yet fail to receive, because you ask with wrong purpose and evil, selfish motives. Your intention is [when you get what you desire] to spend it in sensual pleasures.

> **Implication:** 4. You [are like] unfaithful wives [having illicit love affairs with the world and breaking your marriage vow to God]! Do you not know that being the world's friend is being God's enemy? So whoever chooses to be a friend of the world takes his stand as an enemy of God.

> **God's Helper:** 5. Or do you suppose that the Scripture is speaking to no purpose that says, "The Spirit Whom He

has caused to dwell in us yearns over us and He yearns for the Spirit [to be welcome] with a jealous love?" But He gives us more and more grace (power of the Holy Spirit, to meet this evil tendency and all others fully). That is why He says, God sets Himself against the proud and haughty, but gives grace [continually] to the lowly (those who are humble enough to receive it).

His Way: 7. So be subject to God. Resist the devil [stand firm against him], and he will flee from you. Come close to God and He will come close to you. [Recognize that you are] sinners, get your soiled hands clean; [realize that you have been disloyal] wavering individuals with divided interests, and purify your hearts [of your spiritual adultery]. [As you draw near to God] be deeply penitent and grieve, even weep [over your disloyalty]. Let your laughter be turned to grief and your mirth to dejection and heartfelt shame [for your sins]. Humble yourselves [feeling very insignificant] in the presence of the Lord, and He will exalt you [He will lift you up and make your lives significant].

An Initial Consideration of Justice:

There are some very interesting philosophical aspects to the word, justice.

First, it is a word we would not have in our dictionaries if it were not for the fact that we have conflicts, for it is only when in a conflict that we cry out for it! Please pause and ponder on the truth of that sentence.

Second, it is considered a metaphysical proof of the existence of God, as it is one of the attributes of God. (For additional metaphysical proofs, see: *The Heavens Proclaim the Glory,* lessons 11-13, by Fr. Robert Spitzer, *You Tube.*)

Third, justice and righteousness are foundations of the throne of God. [Psalm 89:14.]

Fourth, justice is something God says we can <u>do</u>:

> He has shown you, O man, what is good. And what does the Lord require of you but to do justly, and to love kindness *and* mercy, and to humble yourself *and* walk humbly with your God? [Micah 6:8; I respectfully suggest that if we can't do the second and third of these three, we will never be able to do the first.]

Fifth, justice is something which comes only from God:

> Many crave *and* seek the ruler's favor, but the wise man [waits] for justice form the Lord. [Proverbs 29:26.]

As you consider the word <u>ruler</u> in the passage, think of: President; Bureaucrat; Legislator; Judge or Jury; Pastor; Counselor; Doctor, etc.

Sixth, have you ever heard this statement:

> "Praise God that he does not give us the justice we deserve, but gives us grace and mercy?"

The statement is not God's whole Truth; His whole Truth is that He <u>does</u> give us justice <u>when</u> we walk His path in dealing with a conflict.

Because I know these truths when I am talking with a person who is in conflict, I run the things they are saying and disclosing about themself through the rolodex of my brain and what I think I know about God and His Christ. (For the younger Reader, you need to Google *Rolodex* to get the visual picture.)

In some cases I work with people who declare themselves to be a Christian, and in some cases people who make no such declaration. Yet almost all at first draw back from dealing with their conflict according to what I tell them about God's Word and Ways.

However, as I proceed I find declared unbelievers significantly more willing to follow God's Way than Believers, often because of the non-believers' past negative experiences with the courts, and the economic benefit they saw in the services of a "voluntary contribution" option.

As I probed the Believers to try to discover why they drew back, I discovered six things to be in play:

1. They **feared** God punishing them for their failures, indicating to me that they had an image of God as "an angry judge".

2. They **feared** that confession and/or forgiveness would lead to their being taken advantage of, particularly if later called into the courts for their actions; i.e., their trust and faith in God was weak, and they could not understand how His *salom* could overcome the damage they believed awaited them.

3. They **thought** that the most fundamental of our legal philosophies of law and system had a Biblical basis, and believed that God's Law (*torah*) was like our modern codes of Crime and Punishment; i.e., they had a false impression of God's *torah* and therefore thought it was proper to use our legal systems.

4. They **thought** our legal system, with its focus on *rights* and *legal protections* (rules of procedure and evidence, burdens of proof, etc) was a safer place to go than to some sort of "church process", but they had no understanding of the pain and agony that would await them in man's legal systems, or of the peace which awaits them along God's path.

5. Believers seemed unimpressed by a possible financial benefit as they expected free stuff from the Church even though the Scripture says: "Let him who receives instruction in the Word [of God] share all good things with his teacher [contributing to his support]." [Galatians 6:6.]

6. Finally, too many religious leaders see the *torah* as being in two parts: one for us individually (the Ten Commandments), and the other required for our corporate structures, justifying full throated support for our legal systems in spite of the warnings of Christ and Paul in Matthew 5:25-26 and I Corinthians 6:7-8. In addition, they too often think of Matthew 18:16 as a trial under Deuteronomy 19:15-21 — which it is not, as we will see later.

Each of these mental impressions impedes our walking God's path when in conflict; thus each must be overcome by reminding ourselves of the proper image of God.

Nine Reasons for this Book

I. To show that to the extent we believe the most fundamental propositions of our Criminal, Tort and Contract laws are Biblically based, it all comes from a misreading of the *torah*, and a misunderstanding of the very nature of God.

II. To show the product of our legal system is anger, bitterness and division, while God's Way for dealing with conflicts offers an opportunity to appropriate His "peace which passes all understanding" (*ergo,* Justice), and find reconciliation with God and man.

III. To give praise and glory to God for His marvelous handbook of *Instructions for Life* (the whole of the Bible) to me, a sinner living life among fellow sinners, in a fallen world.

IV. To show that the <u>purpose</u> of the *torah* for our corporate structures, and His <u>methods</u>, are in total harmony with His Purpose and Methods for His *instructions* to individuals. Both are settings of conflicts, and His way in all conflicts does not change. Thus His Purpose for us to find peace and reconciliation with Him and others when in conflict are present in both categories.

V. To show that it is His *Way* for dealing with conflict which helps distinguish His Instructions from our Law Codes.

VI. To encourage my fellow Believers to first try God's way for dealing with conflict, and to reject the courts and other alternatives of man unless drawn kicking and screaming into them — and then, with Believers daily at our side, to walk only as far as necessary in the court process and then walk only in His Way.

VII. To convey God's *Truth* of what Justice is and is not, why it is founded upon the fact that conflicts will come upon us, why our desire for justice is natural, and how to find His peace and justice when in conflict.

VIII. To show the reader how I have *proven* Proverbs 29:26 and Micah 6:8 to be trustworthy <u>when I look</u> to Him for justice, <u>wait</u> upon Him for it, and <u>actually do</u> the justice He sets before me in my conflict(s) of the moment.

IX. To remind Believers of six passages of Scripture, and ask them to keep these in the forefront of their minds as they read on:

> **Romans 8:1** Therefore, [there is] now no <u>condemnation</u> (no adjudging guilty of wrong) for those who are in Christ Jesus, *who live [and] walk not after the dictates of the flesh, but after the dictates of the Spirit* [John 3:18.]

> **Romans 8:15** For [the Spirit which] you have now received [is] not a Spirit of slavery to put you once more in bondage to **fear**, but you have received the Spirit of adoption [the Spirit producing son-ship] in [the bliss of] which we cry, Abba (Father)! Father!

> **Romans 8:28** We are assured *and* know that [God being a partner in their labor] all things work together *and* are [fitting into a plan] for good to *and* for those who love God and are called according to [His] design *and* purpose.

> **Romans 8:38-39** For I am persuaded beyond doubt (am sure) that neither death nor life, nor angels nor principalities, nor things impending *and* threatening nor things to come, nor powers, nor height nor depth, nor anything else in all creation will be able to separate us from the love of God which is in Christ Jesus our Lord.

> **I John 4:18** There is no **fear** in love [dread does not exist], but full-grown (complete, perfect) love turns **fear** out of doors, *and* expels every trace of **terror**! For **fear** brings with it the thought of **punishment**, and [so] he who is **afraid** has not reached the full maturity of love [is not yet grown into love's complete perfection].

> **I Peter 3:10-12a** Let him who wants to enjoy life and see good days [good — whether apparent or not] keep his tongue free from evil and his lips from guile (treachery, deceit). Let him turn away from wickedness *and* shun it, and let him do right. Let him search for peace (harmony;

undistrubedness from fears, agitating passions, and moral conflicts) and seek it eagerly. [Do not merely desire peaceful relations with God, with your fellowmen, and with yourself, but <u>pursue, go after them</u>!] For the eyes of the Lord are upon the righteous (those who are upright and in right standing with God), and His ears are attentive to their prayer.

My Journey to and with God

Although there was never a day in my life in which I did not know that God existed, that I was responsible to Him, and that Jesus was His Son who died for me, my life <u>with</u> God began in the 9th month of my life as a Judge — September, 1977, at age 36. As a Judge, God convicted me of being a sinner by nature, in need of a Savior.

As I continued on as Judge, I increasingly ran into impediments of the Law stopping me from doing what I thought was my duty as a judge; i.e., "to do justice". My response to my dilemma was to try to compel the law to live up to its promises.

The places where the dilemma most often presented itself were: Criminal Court; Juvenile Court; and Civil Mental Health Commitments. The reasons why it came up in those areas were: mandatory sentences in Criminal Court; and, a lack of funding of the State's "statutory promises" associated with all three areas as other priorities were allowed to steal the resources.

My first conflict came when I was forced to apply the mandatory sentencing provisions of Indiana's Criminal Code. There were several reasons for this.

Indiana was the first state to fall into the trap of thinking that judges were too lenient.

I had been Chairman of the Indiana Board of Correction before becoming judge, and vividly recalled the Commissioner of Corrections telling the legislature: "If you pass these amendments to our laws, you will increase the prison population by 50% in 10-years." He was slightly wrong; if I recall correctly, it doubled in 5-years.

But in the criminal justice area, our primary problem is that we believe we can deter crime via punishment, a totally false premise. So when we don't see deterrence happening, we believe the "lenient judges" are impeding the goal of deterrence and must be restricted in sentencing abilities, and increase the level of punishment. This perceived leniency is another false premise, and I participated in a judicial study which proved that.

In a Mandatory Sentencing State, the Legislature — without ever meeting an individual offender, or reading their pre-sentence report – compels incarceration for a fixed minimum period of time based upon the name and material elements of a particular crime, and the history of the offender.

> Example: Use of a implement capable of causing injury, and using it to cause injury (even if that injury is merely pain), is an aggravated form of assault and battery which makes any sentence non-suspendable; i.e., probation is not an option.

> A man stood before me charged with striking a police officer with a lead pencil, breaking off the tip of the pencil in the officer's hand, causing pain. The minimum, mandatory penalty was 6-years; upper limit was 20-years.

I think I was unduly sensitive to the issue of mandatory sentences because: (a) I had studied penology while chairman of the Board of Correction; (b) my studies had led me to look at the Juvenile Justice, Mental Health, and Special Education systems which seemed to feed the prisons; and, (c) I was the father of a child with special-ed needs which we had to purchase on the open market as the State had not funded its Special Education law at that time.

I also knew that the Indiana Constitution said the following:

> The penal code shall be founded on the principles of reformation, and not of vindictive justice [Article I, Bill of Rights, Section 18],

Finally, by the time I launched my battle with the legal system over mandatory sentences, I had already served a year as a Criminal, Juvenile, and Mental Health judge, so I had additional judicial experiences to add to my book of "Life Lessons".

In January, 1978, I declared the mandatory sentencing statutes unconstitutional on multiple legal theories. I released a man from prison after one year when the mandatory sentence was an indeterminate 10-20 years.

After nearly a year of his freedom, the Indiana Supreme Court, on appeal by the prosecutor, declared the mandatory sentences constitutional because of a "savings clause" in its statute, and ordered me to send the man back to prison.

I reacted (shall I be bluntly honest?) very, very injudiciously.

In early 1981, I was found in Indirect Criminal Contempt of the Indiana Supreme Court for my reaction; that is the story in *Loving God*.

I left the Bench in February, 1982, while facing formal charges to be removed and disbarred. I left not because of that threat, but because I felt God asking me to leave rather than fight a fight I wanted to fight.

It was then that I surrendered to Christ as my Lord for life in all matters, and resigned. I returned to the practice of law for 18 months, during which time, to my surprise, the charges against me for loss of license were dismissed by the Indiana Supreme Court, and the man was granted early release.

> **Lesson learned**: Because I felt God asked me to resign, *and I did what He asked*, I found myself at peace with God and man, even though I felt it would have been *unjust* to remove me from the Bench and take my license away.

> **Lesson not learned**: While I found peace with God, I was not at peace with our system, and had not yet understood God's wisdom as to Justice; thus *injustices* still nagged at my soul. Three years later, I saw my original errors. That allowed me to see the process against me, and its result, as legally and Godly appropriate. I also saw that I was seeking vindication, and that vindication, like Justice, comes only from God. I apologized to the Supreme Court by letter and to the people by newspaper interview — and full peace flooded over me.

During those 18 months, I had a number of people come to me charged with crimes and wanting me to represent them. In all instances I asked them if they had done the acts charged. While most attorneys don't ask that question, I felt compelled to ask it. With two exceptions, all said that had done the acts charged.

I would then tell them their "rights", explain how the legal system works, including through plea and sentence bargaining, and the sentence possibilities. But I went on to share with them the *emotional and spiritual prison* I had just been in for a year as I fought against *the laws of man*. I warned them of creating their own *prison* by denial of their improper acts, and encouraged them to plead guilty without any effort to *plea-bargain* or avoid the legal consequences of their acts. [*see,* I Corinthians 6:7-8 and Matthew 5:25-26 on this reality.]

What I was doing, unconsciously and without asking if they were a Believer, was to share Truths of God as I had come to understand them in the time since the contempt charges were first filed. [*see,* II Corinthians. 1:3-5.]

Amazingly, all but two accepted the Truths and pled guilty with no bargaining. They also found peace in the process, regardless of the consequences (sentences) imposed.

The two who did not plead guilty, and whom I came to believe had not done the acts charge, both went to trial, were convicted, and sent to prison. One deserved to be there, but not for the charged crime; I remain uncertain about the other.

In 1983, I left law (I thought for life), and Ellen and I (and our two younger sons) moved to Minnesota where we took over leadership of CCS-MN. There we studied what the Bible has to say about conflict, how to deal with it, how to help others who are in it, and the role of the Body of Christ in *one-anothering one another,* a/k/a, *discipling.* We learned it, taught it, and served people in conflict through I Corinthians 6:1-6 and Matthew 18:12-20 processes.

We were not alone in this, as a number of youngish attorneys were dropping out and starting these services in the late '70's and through the '80's. Our "small group meetings" were by long distance phone calls – which we had to pay for in those ancient days.

After 4+ years with CCS of MN, we left believing God had called us to become itinerants of this ministry of reconciliation wherever He would lead [*see,* II Corinthians 5:14-21]. Thinking we might well starve in the process, thinking it would help to be debt free, being empty-nesters and lusting to get back to the Rockies where we had met and married, we found a piece of land in SW Colorado and built a home by our own hands — with the help of our three sons and some people God graciously brought into our lives at the time.

During the following 6-years (1988-1993), we took day-labor jobs as available, and went wherever He sent us. In the process, we immersed ourselves into His Ways for dealing with conflict, making it a part of our everyday life. In so doing, we appropriated His Ways in our own conflicts, and found they resulted in our finding both peace and justice!

By 1992, I had come to a number of additional conclusions about law and justice:

> **A. Justice is a word we would not have in our vocabularies were it not for the fact that we have conflicts, for it is only when in a conflict that the word jumps into our mind, unbidden.**
>
> **B. The concept of Justice is also a metaphysical proof of the existence of a God-Creator who is Just and who writes such a concept on our hearts before birth.**
>
> **C. We <u>do</u> Justice by confessing to God our acts which have hurt others, confessing them to those whom we have hurt, and then doing, as led by the Spirit, what we can at the moment to help make things right.**
>
> **D. We <u>do</u> Justice by forgiving others of their acts which have hurt us, and by seeking a new and transformed relationship with them.**
>
> **E. We <u>do</u> Justice by sharing these Truths with others who are in conflict, and by helping them along their path to His Justice, bearing their burdens as needed [Gal. 6:2].**
>
> **F. We <u>do</u> these things with no expectation of anything other than being able to sleep like a baby — which we did — thereby appropriating His Justice.**
>
> **G. Therefore, I define Justice as: "sleeping like a baby even though the conflict may still swirl or even end poorly!"**

My "proof texts" for these things, in addition to Adam and Eve [Genesis 3] and the *Trial of Shadrach, Meshach, & Abednego vs. Nebuchadnezzar* [Daniel 3], are: Matthew 5:20-26; Matthew 18:12-20; I Corinthians 6:1-8; James 4:1-4; and James 5:13-16.

In 1992 I wrote a pamphlet entitled *Reconsidering and Redefining Justice* [see at: shepherdsforpeace.com] and presented it at an *Alternatives in Sentencing* conference in California to which I had been sent by Colson. I think there were ten people in the room, and except for two from East-Bloc countries, it was a dud. I did not then know why those two were enthralled by it, but I was soon to experience why.

In October, 1993, I received a letter from the *International Institute for Christian Studies* (IICS; now *Global Scholars*), wanting to know if we would consider going somewhere in the world to: (a) teach law and, (b) inculcate God, His Word and His Christ into how we lived and what we taught.

They did suggest we might need some long underwear.

On February 1, 1994, Ellen and I landed in Moscow, in a blizzard. My job description, as supplied by the *Moscow State Open University*, was:

> Teach us the meaning of the Western Words of law, <u>and their moral foundations,</u> because we know that law without a moral foundation is without value.

In order to go, I needed to refresh my recollections of our Anglo-American law, its history, philosophy and methodology. I spent hours and hours reading those *Nutshells*, and the Bible.

When I began my review of the law, I began with that which I knew from growing up in the home of a lawyer/OT scholar in the United States of the '40's and '50's:

> The most fundamental philosophies of our law codes of Crime and Punishment are Biblically based.

Neither my coming to Christ nor surrendering to Him had change that, even though I had determined our systems were not capable of delivering justice except by accident.

And, yes, this was exactly what I found Believers and non- believers voicing when rejecting following God's Word when in their conflicts.

> I sometimes wonder if so many others believe this is because it is so deeply ingrained in the psyche of the average Anglo-American because of our legal history. Such an idea would match Paul's journey of changing his image of God after separating from community for his studies.

In a manner of speaking, I had separated myself during those 10-years in the ministry of reconciliation.

But I can tell you that when I have been among people inclined (because of ethnic, clan, tribal, religious, or hard-environment-to-sustain- life), or forced to practice *one- anothering* because of living under totalitarianism, I have found that they don't have this concept of a legal system delivering justice, for they have no law they could use if they wanted to!

It was during my law-review that my image of God, and construct for life was radically transformed.

As I read the *Nutshells*, I was probably like Paul sitting in the desert and running the *torah* through his mind as he pondered the God Whom he had met on the road instead of the God he was told about growing up under the tutelage of the Pharisees. I wonder how many scrolls he took with him? I took 3, 70-pound boxes of law books to Moscow!

My innards, like I think Paul's, kept saying to me: "Wait! That is not Biblical!"

So I went back to *torah* to see why I was feeling so uncomfortable with my prior construct of God and life.

Exodus 21:22-25 hit like a sledge hammer, for it showed a thought like that in Matthew 18:12-20 where I had been immersed for 10-years. The passage indicates you can't even go to a judge until first speaking with the other(s) involved in your conflict!

I ended up spending as much time in the *torah* as in the *Nutshells* trying to wrap my mind around what I was concluding. And that time, in turn, also allowed me to merge the two philosophies into the classroom.

Why did this new construct take place within me?

It was a consequence of: (a) my years as a child of an activist litigating attorney/politician; (b) practice of law and interest in political matters; (c) being a judge; (d) disgracing myself as judge; (e) finding peace through ownership of my errors and taking steps to do justice relative to my disgrace; and (f) spending 10-years away from law and immersed in God's Ways for Peace.

My recent and "new" mind [Romans 12:1-3] was now filled with passages convincing me that finding and doing peace-justice when in conflict was at the very center of the heart of God; i.e., at the heart of One desiring to show His Creation how to reconcile with Him, and with one another. My pamphlet had been merely a first step, for I had not then stopped to consider how what I was now seeing related to our legal systems as opposed to personal relationships and everyday conflicts.

As I taught students in the former U.S.S.R., encountered their communal-approach to dealing with offenses and life in general, and continued to pour though the Scriptures, I added six more conclusions to my new construct for living life:

H. God's *torah* is not a Criminal Code; it is a set of gracious *instructions* for living life free of the things thrown at us by our own sin, the sins of others, and the World.

I. His *torah* does not operate by pretending to read another's mind for its intent, recklessness, or negligence, and then convicting and punishing them. Instead, it is designed to be worked out in a manner in which we might come to see that our chosen actions have hurt someone, confess, forgive, and do justice — and, so far as it rests with us, find peace with God and man.

J. God is not *punitive* in His essential character, nor blindfolded like *Lady Justice,* nor wielding a two-edged sword to chop us apart. Instead, He allows us to face the consequences of our actions so we might learn more about ourselves and Him, and turn more quickly to Him when in conflict.

K. When God disciplines/chastises us, as would any loving father [Hebrews 12:15-16], it is for this same *Purpose;* i.e., for drawing us closer to Him.

L. God does not judge, discipline or chastise to accomplish *general deterrence* but as a "specific form of instruction of an individual unto greater understanding for the moment", which is like our doctrine of *special deterrence*:

A goal of a specific conviction and sentence to dissuade <u>an offender</u> from committing crimes in the future. [*Black's.*] I believe *special deterrence* may well be a Godly philosophy.

M. The consequences of rejecting God's *Instructions*, and willfully walking away from Him (whether by a Believer or a non-believer) can be, particularly for a Believer, catastrophic to one's enjoyment of *the abundant life* [*see*: I Corinthians 5:1-5], and for the unbeliever, eternal separation from God.

Today, I believe that until a member of the Body of Christ comes to these 12 conclusions, they will jump into the bushes and try to hide when in conflict — instead of drawing near to God, His Word, His Christ, His Spirit, and His People for help.

"Come out of the Bushes!"

Yes, the idea of jumping into the bushes comes from Gen. 3, and I will close this portion of my Brief by looking at that passage – one I am sure you are familiar with.

1. Eve had a conversation with the Serpent <u>while Adam stood there in silence</u>.

Jewish scholars say he was there at the time of the conversation. Why Adam did not take the authority God had given him to tell the serpent to butt out, I do not know — but his silence was to steal from women any sense of protection/security that they desired to have in their husbands.

2. Eve took, ate, and gave some to Adam, who also ate.

Both did a *volitional act*, and not a *reflex reaction act*. <u>And that is the way God judges our acts which hurt</u> — not by accusing our mind or heart, but by laying the truth of our <u>chosen</u> act while asking: "And how should you, at this moment and for this act of yours, go forward in time living before Me, Who has loved you so much as to die for you while you were dead in your sins?"

3. The Universe crashed.

THEY FELT IT, THEY KNEW IT, AND KNEW IT WAS BECAUSE OF THEIR ACT. Their sense of nakedness, and efforts to cloth themselves by the works of their own hands establish those truths. And, of course, it did not work for them, and never will work for anyone.

4. They heard God walking in the Garden, and jumped into the bushes, probably digging like Badgers.

Forget how absolutely dumb this was; just acknowledge you can't hide yourself or the things you do from God.

5. God called out: "Adam, where are you?"

He did not scream this; there was no flashing bubble-gum machine and sirens; there was not even anger — but there may have been a tone of sadness. Yet, miracle of miracles, they came out!

Why did they come out of the bushes?

When you realize you have stepped in the do-do of life, what do you do? Do you immediately take responsibility, confess to those you have hurt, seek to make things right? Or do you hide in the bushes of legalism and start the blame game:

> "I didn't do it; I didn't mean to do it; everyone is doing it; if you were poor, you would do it; Mommy made me do it; Satan made me do it; You, God, did not protect me from it or stop me from doing it or stop someone else from doing it to me;" etc, etc, etc.

Standing in our own do-do creates a pivotal moment in time for us. Our choice about what to do will have a huge impact on us — for good or for ill.

I believe that it is our image of God that will move us onto our future path: out of the bushes towards the foot of the Cross, versus deeper into the bushes of fear, anger, bitterness, rage, disillusionment, despair, and defeat.

Have you ever really thought through what Christ's death on the Cross, and your acceptance of His sacrifice means? Of the *position* it has given you *in Christ Jesus* before God the Father for your times of conflict and troubles?

You are in the hand of Christ, and "no one is able to snatch them out of My hand." Jesus said He only has you because the Father gave you to

Him, "and no one is able to snatch them out of the Father's hand, for I and the Father are One." [John 10:27-30.]

Adam and Eve did not have the benefit of our theological understanding of today, nor the Scriptures, nor the sign of the Cross, nor the indwelling Holy Spirit.

Yet they came out of the bushes, albeit heads hanging and blaming the serpent, one another, and God. So, why did they come out?

It is the question most related to what I want to convey to you about God, so let me tell you why they came out, and invite you to take the same path when you are in a conflict.

We assume Adam must have been at least a late teenager when, poof, he was in existence. Written on his heart were things of God his Creator, i.e., the "Image of God". Did these include "these commandments which I commend you this day" [Deuteronomy. 30:11-14]? I don't know.

Did it include "the conscience"? Yes, and maybe nothing more. After all, Adam had to learn the names of the animals (yeah, I think God already knew them, but invited Adam into the creative process), but how did Adam learn anything else about anything else?

Yes, he learned by trial and error, but how did he gain *wisdom* and *understanding* from his trials and errors?

I suggest that everything Adam and Eve "knew" about anything whatsoever that had to do with living "life" had come from having walked and talked directly with God.

AND IT HAD ALL BEEN GOOD — even the one instruction which they chose to reject!

So there they were, hiding in the bushes, and fully aware that the works of their own hands (making clothing from fig leaves) was of no value when it came to being in the presence of, or relationship with, God.

I suggest that they paused and thought for a moment.

Pausing to consider what you know of God in the first instant of the beginning of a conflict — or first

awareness of a conflict which has been raging for a long time — is the best possible thing you can do!

Adam and Eve did it, **and then remembered that it had all been good, VERY, VERY GOOD!**

In this respect, they are exactly like the story of the Prodigal Son which Jesus told [Luke 15:11-32, particularly 17-18]: "Then when he came to himself, **and recalled the nature of his Father**, he said "I will get up and go to my father."

Thus Adam and Eve, with their limited knowledge, and in simple trust, came out to face the music, **trusting Him Who is *Good* to also *DO GOOD*.**

They knew not what their future was, nor what His *doing good* might mean, but they knew He was A Good Creator, and had experienced His Goodness.

A moment ago I said that I had concluded that God is not punitive in His essential nature. Rather he allows man to face the consequences of his actions, including building a Hell on Earth for himself today — and forever by their ongoing and forever rejection of Him.

You want to know part of why I believe that?

It is simple. Here is what would have happened if God were focused on punishing Adam and Eve to deter us in the future from disobeying Him:

> God would have hung Adam and Eve from a tree, made a new Adam and Eve, and taken them on a tour of the Garden ending at where the two of them hung. There He would have pointed to the bodies and said: "Don't eat from that tree which I told you not to eat from, or that will be you."

That is man's philosophy and way. That is *general deterrence*, which creates only bondage to fear within us. That is not Biblical.

And when the 2nd Adam and Eve would eat (or do something else contrary to God's *Instructions*), they would have jumped into the bushes — and they would all still be hiding there, along with all of us, if God does not come down to call them forth.

Dear Believers, we on this side of the Cross have no excuse for thinking God is waiting to zap us.

We have no spiritual reason to hide in the bushes when we step in the do-do.

God, His Word and Spirit are screaming at us:

COME OUT! THERE IS A WAY FORWARD!
(*see,* Romans 7:21 to Romans 8:39)

Yet we forget His goodness, and in futility try to hide and avoid dealing with things according to His instructions.

Why?

Is it possibly because we see God through a lens of the false *theology* of our Penal Code and Criminal Justice *philosophies* — just as Paul saw God through a false lens of his specific time, place, and people — and thus we fear God even more than man?

An Interesting View of Law and Religion

Why might the philosophies of man in our Criminal Code be so powerful when we are in even a very simple conflict?

Rousas John Rushdoony said this in his *Institutes of Biblical Law* (Presbyterian and Reformed Publishing, 1984, @ pg 4 and following):

> Law is, in every culture, *religious in origin*. Because law governs man and society, because it establishes and declares the meaning of justice and righteousness, law is inescapably religious in that it establishes in practical fashion the ultimate concerns of a culture....
>
> *Second*, it must be recognized that in any culture *the source of law is the god of that society*. If law has its source in man's reason, then reason is the god of that society. If the source is an oligarchy, or in a court, senate, or ruler, then that source is the god of that system....
>
> Modern humanism, the religion of the state, locates law in the state and thus makes the state the god of the system. ...
>
> [WDB: This was the precise position of Russia throughout the Great Proletariat Revolution, and the compelled belief of its people lest they disappear into the Gulags.]
>
> *Third*, in any society, any change of the law is an explicit or implicit change of religion....
>
> *Fourth*, no disestablishment of religion as such is possible in any society. A church can be disestablished, and a particular religion can be supplemented by another, but the change is simply to another religion. Since the foundations of law are inescapably religious, no society

exists without a religious foundation or without a law-system which codifies the morality of its religion.

Fifth, there can be no tolerance in a law-system for another religion. Toleration is a device used to introduce a new law-system as a prelude to a new intolerance.... Every law-system must maintain its existence by hostility to every other law-system and to alien religious foundations, or else it commits suicide.

[WDB: Can you now comprehend why the U.S. is so sharply and viciously divided today between the Christians and our Nation acting through its courts?]

In analyzing now the nature of Biblical law, it is important to note *first* that, for the Bible, law is revelation. The Hebrew word for law is *torah*, which means *instruction, authoritative direction*. The Biblical concept of law is broader than the legal codes of the Mosaic formulation. It applies to the divine word and instruction in its totality.

I have suggested that "We the People" have imported into God's *torah* philosophical principles of our Criminal and Penal Codes, and that the Organized Church and Believers have accepted those propositions as God's Truths.

But these 1000-year old principles are not God's Truths!

Because we think they are, we are willing to go to law like the unbeliever, expecting justice from a system when it comes only from God! [*see*, Proverbs 29:26.]

Worse, we are willing to reject His Instructions even for the most mundane things of daily life [*see*, I Corinthians 6:1-6]. Worst of all, we may reject God's Ways out of fear of God when we stumble and fall.

I believe that if you know how the tainted philosophies entered into our laws and legal systems, and see them compared to God's Ways for dealing with conflict, it will help you reject man's systems when in conflict and encourage you to seek after God's Ways.

Therefore, it is time to look into our legal history.

It began in the age of Feudalism [8th Century], in England. From its beginnings to the coming of William the Conqueror in 1066 AD, that system, which was based on contract, put into motion three portions of our modern law: Contract Law; Property Law (Real and Personal property), and Inheritance.

However, conflicts of the people among themselves were dealt with by informal processes in each community, as there were no courts as we know that term. We will look at examples of community processes as we move along.

In 1066, William conquered all of southern England. To forge the feudal Barons into a modern State, William declared those community squabbles to be threats to the King's Peace [i.e., crimes] and created courts and Shire-Reeves [sheriffs] to arrest, try, convict and punish the breaker of the Law, the breaker of the "King's Peace". It was during the transformation that the deceits of Satan got into our Western Law Philosophies; we will get to them in a moment.

By 1215, the Barons were tired of kings being kings and doing more harm than good. They rebelled and forced King John to sign *Magna Carta*. The next year they secured the *Charter of the Forest*, giving back to the people all their historic right of access to, and use of the forests as common lands prior to King John. These two documents, along with the 1627 *Petition of Rights*, the 1688 *Bill of Rights*, and the *Habeas Corpus Act of 1679*, reminded a wayward King of the rights of an Englishman, and form the basis for the Common Law and a constitution in England today – for it has no single written document entitled "Constitution".

If you wonder what a *Petition* or *Bill of Rights* was, read our Declaration of Independence; it followed the ancient blueprint in reminding King George III of his errors.

About 1470 AD — 600-years after the start of Feudalism; 400- years after William and the initial development of the philosophy for our Criminal Law; 250-years after *Magna Carta*; and 320 years before the adoption of the U. S. Constitution — Sir John Fortescue [c. 1394-1479), Chief Justice of the King's Bench of England], wrote a book entitled *In Praise of the Laws of England* (trans. by Francis Gigor, London, 1917). It was written for the instruction of young Prince Edward, heir apparent to the throne. When the young prince showed himself reluctant to consider the book, Justice Fortescue interlineated this comment:

But Sir, how will you have righteousness and justice unless you first acquire a competent knowledge of the law by which justice is to be learned and known?

Do you see the lie, the twist from God as Source of Justice to man and his law as source? For 550-years we have bought into and lived that lie!

[*In Praise of the Laws of England, Chpt. 5, "Igorance of the Law Causes a Contempt Thereof* (transl. by Francis Gigor, London, 1917).]

[Quoted from, *The Nature and Functions of the Law*, Dr. Harold J. Berman, Foundation Press (1958), @ pg 4. Dr. Berman was the James Barr Professor of Law, Harvard University; Robert W. Woodruff Professor of Law, Emory University School of Law; and an expert in comparative, international and Soviet-Russian law as well as legal history, the philosophy of law, and the intersection of law and religion.]

Now "the law" to which Fortescue referred was the Law of England, not the Law of God. Yet it was common knowledge then that the maker's of English Law back in the period following William the Conqueror drew thoughts for their legal system from the Bible. Thus, in the mind of the people, the law of England was like unto the Law of God.

Another word for such a situation is *an idol*; another is *heresy*.

This was so inbred by 1470 that Fortescue could declare that man's law was the source of justice and righteousness!

As I said, for 550-years we have bought into this heresy.

By "we", I include myself, the organized church, the vast majority of Believers, the whole of our nation, and much of the World.

A Lesson Learned from a Collective-Minded People:

In 2002, I was sitting at a Round Table in Astana, the modern capital of Kazakhstan. There were 25 experts of the law at the table: Minister of Justice; the President's special envoy on Justice; members of parliament; teachers of law, political science, philosophy, criminology, penology; Ministers of the police and military; etc., etc.

The Kazakh Criminal Code had, in their opinion, become too harsh, and they wanted to pick the brain of a Western "man of the law" about how to deal with the perceived harshness. Please note that deep down they knew general deterrence was not only not working, but was producing unnecessary harm.

We have yet to understand those two things, and until we consider them there is little chance of meaningful reform to our laws and systems.

The first thing they brought up was our Plea and Sentencing Bargaining system. They thought it might ameliorate the harshness, even though they already had a provision in their law which said "if an offender acknowledges their wrong, any penalty cannot exceed 50% of the statutory maximum."

By reading from my Bible, I explained to them why, if they were interested of having an appearance of justice and a finding of peace they should not walk our path. They grasped the theology immediately, and cast the idea aside. [Half the table would see themselves as of Islam; the other half, of Russian Orthodoxy, but few had more than "folk religion".]

Their second issue involved another provision of their Criminal Code: "If an offender reconciles with his victim by giving the victim what the victim desires, there is no criminality for the act." This had been their law for hundreds of years, yet they could not understand it in this era of big cities and skyscrapers.

I outlined God's way for dealing with conflict, and applied it to criminal legal philosophy and method. You can find two examples of this: one at *R. v. Moses*:

https://www.canlii.org/en/yk/yktc/doc/1992/1992canlii12804/1992 canlii12804.html?autocompleteStr=1992%2071%20C.C.C.%20(3d)%20 347&autocompletePos=1

and the other by Googling, *Justice in the Community: The New Zealand Experiment*. Both of these incorporate God's theology, one part of which involves removing fault (intent, recklessness, and negligence) from the system, and replacing it with strict liability, thereby focusing on the act done and not the state of the mind of the actor – but with a totally different mechanism utilized, which mechanism offers an opportunity to get right with God and man, and find peace and justice.

Their leading professor on the subject immediately said: "But it is impossible to have a criminal justice system without *fault*." Yet after some discussion and contemplation, the Nation of Kazakhstan amended their law codes to allow for mediation of criminal cases!

Another Interesting View
of Law and Religion

The Hon. Harlan F. Stone (1872-1946) [Dean of Columbia Law School; Attorney General of the U.S.; one time Associate and Chief Justice of the U.S. Supreme Court], said the following about the need of the average individual to have a certain knowledge and understanding of the laws of his or her Nation in order to be a good and participating member of his nation:

> [pg iii] "... Law lies at the very root of civilization itself, for science, art, commerce, the capacity of cooperative effort by communities and peoples which we identify with civilization, have become possible only through the establishment of social order, which in turn makes law possible, and of which law is the necessary concomitant. . . . there are certain fundamental notions of the nature of law, certain facts relating to its history and development, and certain principles which underlie its efficient administration which should become a part of the intellectual equipment of every intelligent citizen." [*Law and Its Administration*, Columbia University Lectures, New York, 1924), pp. 1-2.]

[Quoted by Dr. Harold Berman in *The Nature and Functions of the Law*, pgs iii.]

First, note that "Social Order" precedes "Law".

I suggest Social Order springs from relationship, and descends into chaos because of the universal presence of sin. We then produce Law in an effort to limit and respond to that descent and chaos. That is why Judge Stone said: "of which law is the necessary concomitant [naturally accompanying result]."

But the old Social Order [community circle] always remains an option when we are willing, and or forced to turn to it.

We in the U.S. see this willingness to submit to Law as necessity, and the essence of "Rule of Law", because we have a role in production of the law. The people of the old USSR knew their Law to be the tool of the totalitarian holding them back, and thus had no willingness to submit to it; and so they lived life in open violation of the law as the only way they could see to survive.

But they also created conflict resolution mechanisms so they would not war against one another while collectively trying to survive as outlaws.

Second, what Justice Stone does not say is how little of Law one actually needs when Social Orderliness is a principle of life applied to conflicts. The former Soviet Union had Social Order *via* the *Collective*, which existed because the existing law was of no benefit to the individual. Let me give you another example:

Another Lesson Learned from a Collective-Mind People:

I was walking with Vaghan (the attorney who made the invitation which landing me in Moscow) when, out of the corner of my eye, I saw an auto collision. The cars veered to the side, stopped, both men got out, and started heading quickly for each other.

> "Vaghan," I said, "looks like trouble." He looked at me as though I was from Mars, and said: *"Ne problema."* [You can translate that.] Sure enough, the men met, and started talking.

> "Vaghan," I said, "what's happening?"

> "Bill, do you see the *militzia* standing down there?" Sure enough, there he was, in his uniform, complete with AK-47 – and he was *watching* the two men.

> "Well, he has the ability to come over and determine who is at fault and assess damages, but only if invited over. [Sounded like a Shire Reeve to me.] But he won't be invited, and he won't come unless violence erupts. And he will not be invited, because if invited, when he gets there, the first thing he will demand are our papers: *propiska* (internal passport *cum* national identity card), vehicle

documents, and work book (from first day of work to death, and required to be on our person at all times), etc."

"Okay", say I, "so he can be judge, jury and executioner all in one – right?" "Yes." "And they won't call him because???"

"Because none of us live where our *propiska* says we live, there are probably no papers for the car, my Work Book may have a Wolf-Stamp in it declaring me to all as a troublemaker and thus I have no job and it is a crime to have no job, and someone will end up in the *gulag*; that is why. You see, everything we do day by day to survive is illegal, so we have to act on a different set of beliefs; i.e., we have to learn to survive in community, while surrounded by the insanity of the government and its worthless law. Welcome to *Moskva*!"

About then, one handed the other some money, they shook hands, and went their separate ways. "Vaghan,", I said, "you don't carry enough money around to pay such damages; tell me more."

"Well", he said, "they decided who was at fault, how much should be paid, and the one made a promise to do so and made a down payment." I laughed; I'm sorry, but I am too conditioned not to.

Vaghan chided me: "Don't laugh; the promise will be kept, for otherwise, we all die."

I believe this is the way God desires that we act, particularly within the Body of Christ, but also, so far as it is possible with us, in matters involving outsiders.

Professor Berman then went on to quote Hon. James Wilson (1742-1798) [lawyer; writer; signatory of the U.S. Declaration of Independence; member of the 1787 Constitutional Convention; Professor of Law at the

University of Pennsylvania; and Associate Justice of the U.S. Supreme Court] from his *Lectures on Law* (1790-1791) [*Works* (Phila., 1804, p. 9)]) for the following statements:

> [pg 4] "The science of law should, in some measure, and in some degree, be the study of every free citizen, and of every free man.... The knowledge of those rational principles on which the law is founded ought, especially in a free government, to be diffused over the whole community.

>> WDB: Right now let me note that while God may be considered a *rational being*, and we were created in His image, our alleged *rationality* is horribly warped by sin. I actually do not believe that our essential principles of fault, punishment and deterrence are *rational*; but, then, I am looking at them through a Biblical lens.

> "... We need laymen who understand the necessity for law and the right uses of it too well to be unduly impatient of its restraints," [Woodrow] Wilson stated. The function of a college course in law, he said, is to teach the student "what law is, how it came into existence, what relation it bears to its substance, and how it gives to society its fiber and strength and poise of frame."

>> **WDB: No; it is God and His Christ who gives us our "fiber and strength and poise (graceful and elegance) of frame."**

Finally, Professor Berman, a devout Believer who integrated his faith and beliefs into his writings, gave us some of his own thoughts:

> [pg 6] ... As our society has grown more urbanized and our law ways more complex, young men have had progressively fewer opportunities to learn about the workings of our legal systems; at the same time the United States has become

probably the most law-run and lawyer-run country in the history of mankind. In addition, the United States is one of the few civilized countries in which the study of law is not undertaken by a substantial proportion of undergraduates, regardless of their professional aspirations.

The reasons for law study in the liberal arts curriculum may be stated in the most elementary terms, therefore, of the need for overcoming sheer ignorance and misinformation on the part of otherwise educated people about a subject of the greatest political, economic and social importance. Not only our educational system but also our legal system suffers. To paraphrase [Georges Benjamin] Clemenceau (1841-1929) [politician; physician; journalist; Prime Minister of France)] – law is too important to be left to the lawyers. Beyond this, the need for such study may be stated in terms of the following propositions...:

a. An understanding of the nature of the legal order and of legal reasoning is of significant cultural value in itself.
b. An understanding of law is essential to an understanding of the political values of American society and of the international community, and it enriches not only political science but also other disciplines such as philosophy, history, economics, sociology, and anthropology.
c. The diffusion of an understanding of law to wider segments of the scholarly community can result in a greater illumination of legal science, as scholars of other disciplines come to give more attention to legal data.
d. The study of law can be an important means of developing the student's sense of justice and his capacity for responsible judgment.

A Proposition and an Ultimate Question

Proposition: If all of the statements from these mighty men of the law are true as to the need for one to have knowledge of the law of *his nation* in order to be a good citizen, then it must also be true that a citizen of the Kingdom of God must have a correct understanding of God, and a willingness to practice His *Instructions* to be able to truly live life in a fallen world – particularly when we are constantly beset by internal and external conflicts.

Ultimate Question: If our understanding of God's *Law* (words originally written in the Hebrew-Aramaic "picture language," and later in Greek) have been skewed from His *Truth* by our translating into the Bible the legal philosophies of our Anglo-American forefathers in Law as if they were God-blessed, where does that leave the citizen of God?

> **It leaves him/her able to change their understanding of God's *torah* by reconsidering their image of God — as did Paul and as have I — and come out of the bushes when in conflict.**

As we go forward, remember that the Bible, at the time of William the Conqueror, was in Latin for the West, where Rome had developed significant legal doctrines and practices

My Rejection of a "Works Unto Salvation" Theology:

I now want to try to establish the truth of my twelve conclusions. However, as this is a legal brief, and someone might read me as arguing God's Law as a *works-theology*, I want to make a few things very clear:

First, I consider God's *Torah*, and I mean the totality of His Holy Scriptures, to be one of His greatest acts of grace to the Fallen World.

> His disclosure of Himself and His *Nature* was His first act,
> and it was all Adam and Eve had to go on.

His Old Testament written Word was His second act.
His crucified and Resurrected Son was His third act.
His Indwelling Holy Spirit was His fourth act.
His New Testament Words were His fifth act.
And His Body of Christ [*ekklesia*] was His sixth act.

**All OF THESE ACTS WERE/ARE ACTS OF GRACE.
WE NEED THEM ALL WHEN IN CONFLICT. AND
WE WILL GET NONE FROM THE LAWS OR LAW-
COURTS OF MAN!**

Second, any search of His *Torah* which I do in order to feel *justified* before Him, is worthless. It is only by His Grace through Christ on the Cross that I am justified.

Third, having been *justified* by Grace, I must now learn [Romans 12:1-3] how to truly live; that is, there is a process called *application of the full Word of God to the Old Man to Live in Newness of Life*. This is known as *sanctification,* a process never completed this side of Glory. This process can't take place *by my flesh* alone, but only by my submission to and working with the Holy Spirit living within me; i.e., I *work* it out in *fear* and *trembling,* and *cooperation.* [*see,* Philippians 2:12.]

Fourth, since Satan can appear as an angel of light, and my "old man" is alive and well in me, I will always be subject to conflicting signals, impulses, and emotions.

Fifth, therefore, when in conflict, I must seek out God's *torah* for help – His gracious "good food" for living life. I do not seek this out to use against another, but only as a "lamp unto my feet." [*see,* Psalm 119.] To grasp this last sentence, I beg of you to take time to read and ponder upon Psalm 119 – "The Psalm of the Law" – for it was the psalmist's "Hymn of Praise to God for His *torah*", and not a hymn to the Law of Man as understood by Fortescue.

In short, as a sinner living among sinners in a universe warped by sin, I need His gracious *instructions* to know how to live at peace.

PRAISE GOD HE HAS PROVIDED THEM TO ME AND YOU!

Lessons Learned from Biblical Linguistics

> *Linguistics* (noun): the scientific study of language and its structure, including the study of <u>morphology</u>, syntax, phonetics, and semantics Specific branches of linguistics include sociolinguistics, dialectology, psycholinguistics, computational linguistics, historical-comparative linguistics, and applied linguistics. (Google Dictionary.)

To see if it is possible for us to have been reading our Bibles improperly, allow me to show you some examples which should help you at least accept that morphing is a possibility.

Morph: verb. 1. Change smoothly from one image to another by small gradual steps using computer animation. [Google translate].

You see, it all comes down to what *torah* [OT] and *no'mos*[NT] meant when they were written into the original scrolls of the Bible.

Until 1611 when the King James' Authorized Version of the Bible was finished and made available to the people, the Bible was in Latin in the West, and Greek in the East. This was:

> 150-years <u>after</u> Sir John Fortescue had equated *justice* with England's law,

> 400-years <u>after</u> *Magna Carta* tried to rein in the King, and,

> 545-years <u>after</u> William the Conqueror created the basic philosophy of our Criminal Code, and stole the conflicts of the people from their communities and into his State Courts — reaping a financial benefit in the process.

That is a lot of time to allow linguistics to *morph* — particularly when the Master Deceiver is at work in the World. So the twist as to the Source of *Justice* by the time of Sir John Fortescue was really no big deal.

Originally, of course, the Old Testament was written in Hebrew-Aramaic, whose words presented a picture of something to the reader. The ancient manuscripts were then translated into the Greek Septuagint 130- years prior to Christ. The New Testament was written in Hebrew and/or Greek, which Rome rewrote into Latin, and on and on it has gone.

But in writing both Testaments, the writers used words as they were understood in the popular meaning of their day, albeit as informed by revelation from God. Thus, in all instances the writers presented the God-Spirit breathed *Word* of God in the original text.

Christ "blessed" the Old Testament as fully accurate.

Yet He kept telling the people that they had misunderstood God, and the Spirit of God behind the written *Words*, and that this error had moved their behaviors in the wrong direction, i.e., towards *legalism* and away from *Grace by Faith*.

Thus Jesus Himself established that we must be very careful in all we read in the Scripture to avoid reading into them something not there in the original languages.

For example, *grace by faith without works* was alive and well in the Old Testament, starting in the Garden — but now is not the time to try to prove that. Adam and Eve knew it before anything was written down, and they experienced it. So did Noah, Abraham, Moses and many, many others.

So let's just accept the fact that God does not change. He may give us different tools from time to time, but His *purposes, methods* and *instructions* do not change from their original *Spirit-direction*.

However, when God began His *spoken word* to the people at the foot of the mountain [Exodus 20:1-17], He only got through the first ten items before the people ran in terror from the thundering, lightnings, trumpets, and smoking mountain. The rest was what God spoke only to Moses, who informed the people. [Exodus 20:18-22.]

In that process, *dabar* [*Vine's*, "to speak", Hebrew pg 239], the full truth of God was lost because the Spirit was separated from the people by the people fleeing. Think of it this way: spirit and inflection are not present when the speaker is not present. It is like the old gossip game – things morph as the story is retold.

The presence of the Spirit united with the Word is critical. Ist Corinthians 3:6 puts it this way:

[It is He] who has qualified us [making us to be fit and worthy and sufficient] as ministers *and* dispensers of a new covenant [of salvation through Christ], not [ministers] of the letter (of legally written code) but of the Spirit; for the code [of the Law] kills, but the [Holy] Spirit makes alive.

Bear in mind that *dabar* as a <u>noun</u> carries with it the actual verbal utterance as well as the content, i.e, "<u>the thoughts and will of the speaker</u>". [*Vine's* pg 240-241.]

In the New Testament, in order to recognize "the Word (Christ) became flesh (human, incarnate) and tabernacled among us" (John 1:14), the Hebrew *dabar* was broken into two words: *logos*:

Logos ... an expression of the thought of the speaker; as to God, the revelation of his will; a message from the Lord, delivered with His authority and made effective by His power, the declarer of the word, and a title for the Son of God. [*Vine's*, Greek, pg 683, *word.*]

rhema – the significance of *rhema* (as distinct from *logos*) is exemplified in the injunction to take "the sword of the Spirit, which is the word of God," Ephesians 6:17; here the reference is not to the whole Bible as such, but to the individual scriptures which the Spirit brings to our remembrance for use in time of need, a prerequisite being the regular storing of the mind with Scripture. [*Vine's*, Greek pg 683]

Thus when the writers sat to write the New Testament, I believe they had to deal with the fact that Jesus was constantly saying: "You have heard it said... but I say unto you..." ; i.e., they had to seriously consider what if anything had been *morphed*, and then select words designed to get the original Heart and Mind of God back into the Scriptures.

I believe this was particularly true when they found things which had been wrongly understood because of the influence of culture and our sin-nature.

I make these conclusions in part from linguistics, in part from the fact that the people at Ex. 20:18-22 ran from the face of God after He recited the 10th *teaching* and in part because Jesus was *the Word made flesh*, which allowed *Pure and Total Truth* to be displayed by and through His every spoken *word*, and *action* as witnessed to and by the Disciples.

And so I ask you: Do you react to God's *torah* as a gracious gift to we who are in need, or as a terrorizing criminal code of "do this or I will cut your hand off"?

Allow me to give you three examples of *meaning-morph* which are very relevant to our day, and to this book.

> First, the Hebrew word for *Law* in the Old Testament is *torah*. Its original meaning was not *law*, but "*instruction, or teaching*".

> "The 'instruction' given by God to Moses and the Israelites <u>became known as</u> 'the law' or 'the direction', and quite frequently as 'the Law of the Lord". [*Vine's* @ Hebrew pgs 133-134 (*Strong's* #8451).]

That, my friends, is *morphing*.

If we are wise, we should admit that there is a great difference between the implication of the message conveyed when one says, "the *law* says", versus when one says, "please consider the following as a wise *instruction* on affairs of this life."

> Second, in our English New Testaments, we find the word, *church* [Matthew 16:13-19; Matthew 18:17]. The Greek word was *ekklesia*, while the Church of Rome used the Latin variant, *ecclesia*. When the New Testament was written (1st Century A.D.), *ekklesia* meant:

> *ek* – "out of" – "*klesis*" – "a calling" (*kaleo*, "to call"), was used among the Greeks of *a body of citizens* "gathered" to discuss the *affairs of state*, Acts. 19:39. [*Vine's*, @ Greek pg 42, *Strong's* #1577.]

45

Now for the back-story on "church", showing the reality of how one's choice of words when translating from one language to another can, particularly over time, *morph* a meaning of a passage.

King James was Scottish. On Sundays, Christian Scots went to a building called a *kirk*. *Kirk* was chosen by the scholars to replace *ekklesia-ecclesia* in the writing of the Authorized Version, and anglicized to *church*.

So, *ekkelsia*, which originally described —

> the essential nature of each person in a group of people
> who gather at a time and place for a combined purpose of
> discussing affairs of State [think *"affairs of the Kingdom
> of God relative to daily living"*]

— *morphed* into *a physical building at a given location and only as to those present at the moment*!

But that was not the end of the *morphing*.

From that came the idea that the people of God were safe from attack by Satan when inside a *Kirk*.

But the plain import of Matthew 16:13-19 is that the people of God, led by the Spirit of God, in the name and power of God, and cooperating with God, could kick down the gates of Hell and set captives free! In my opinion, the *morph* destroyed the entire message!

> A Russian Orthodox Church has but one door, on the West
> side of the building. As one leaves through that door, they
> pass under a large mural depicting Christ standing on the
> head of the Serpent, and people running free from Hell!

> The Russians I met understand *ekklesia* very clearly. For
> example, an Orthodox Church has no confessional booth
> or penance routine of payment of something to the church.
> Instead, if you seek guidance from a Priest it is on a bench
> on the side of the sanctuary, in open view of all. When the
> Priest speaks, it will be to talk about the shortcoming you
> have displayed in your confession, followed by instructions
> of acts of confession and forgiveness you should consider
> taking in order to help make things right.

In light of the John 17 passage, and my time in the former U.S.S.R., I phrase *ekklesia* as: "the Body of Christ called out of the world to gather together to help one another live in this world, and to go forth into this world as the hands, feet, tongues *etc* of the Lord, setting captives free." [II Corinthians 1:3-5, and 4:5-7.]

Now for a third example of linguistics – which I hope literally blows you away. The Greek word for *Law* in the New Testament is *nomos*. Paul, the lawyer turned upside down, was looking for a Greek word to equal the original idea of *torah, i.e.,* loving instruction, and so he chose *nomos*:

> *nomus* (Strong's #3551). Akin to *nemo*, "to divide out, **distribute**," primarily meant "that which is assigned": **hence,** "usage, custom." **and then,** "law, law as prescribed by custom, or by statute"; the word *ethos*, "custom," was retained for unwritten "law," while ***nomos* became** the established name for "law" as decreed by a state and set up as a standard for the administration of justice. [*Vines'* Greek at page 354.]

Read the progression of the meaning of the original word carefully. Does it sound like a Fortescue-*morph* to you? It sure does to me.

So let's go back to the start of the *Vines's* statement: "to distribute". Here is what I wanted to know when I first looked at this: **Who is Distributing What, to Whom, for What Purpose?**

Are those not logical questions? Might not the answers tell us more about the operative intent of the selector of the word (God being the selector through Paul and others?)

I asked this to myself because I knew the One Who *distributed gracious instruction* via the *torah* was, is, and ever will be the Creator, Provider, and Sustainer of us all. And I also knew a key purpose for God's *torah*, was Roman's 3:19:

> Now we know that whatever the **Law** says, it speaks to those who are under the **Law**, so that [the murmurs and excuses of] every mouth may be hushed, and all the world may be held accountable to God.

In light of these things, *Strong's Concordance #3551*, for the King James Version, says this of *no'mos*:

> From a primary (to parcel out, **especially food or grazing to animals**); law (<u>through the idea of prescriptive usage</u>), genitive case (regulation), specially, (of Moses (including the volume); also of the Gospel), or figuratively (a principle). Translation: law.
>
> **So, how did we convert, "A Good Shepherd distributing Good Grain to the dumb and stumbling sheep," — an act of grace calling us back to God — into a penal code from which we run in terror?**
>
> **Question**: Did the transformed lawyer Paul, after learning directly from God over a period of years in the wilderness, just casually pick *no'mos*, or did the Spirit make the choice to reestablish the proposition that God's *torah* is not "a code of crime and punishment to deter evil", but "good and necessary grain for living, distributed to the deaf, dumb and blind sinners who accept the Gift of Christ, so that they might know how to live in a fallen world"?

You be the judge.

Man's Law: Source, Purpose, Method, Consequences

Let us look at this from another angle. A philosopher would put it this way:

The *Source* of a thing determines its *Purpose*.
The *Purpose* then determines the *Method*.
The *Method* then produces *Consequences* – good and bad.

Now the *Source* of our Criminal Law, its *Purpose*, *Method*, and *Consequences*, all flow from the Mind of Men, albeit "informed by" study, debate and consensus, including study of God's Word. But *consensus* of that study becomes *the truth* of the participants, and not necessarily *The Truth* of our Maker.

So: "From whence came the idea that we could deter people in general by punishment of a single individual?" Remember, I have said that this is a false doctrine.

At the time of William, what you had was essentially a merged church-state society. The church was "the Church in the West" [Rome], and not "the church of the East" [Orthodox], for they had split in 1054 AD.

The church in Rome had both a confessional booth [from which springs our "right to remain silent"], and penance with payment to the church [which became fines to the State]. Russian Orthodoxy has neither of these, for whatever that tidbit is worth.

Deterrence was based upon two theological propositions, and a Scripture found in many variants and places in the OT:

1. Man is a rational being, having knowledge of good and evil, made in the image of the Creator, and thereby a rational being. [WDB: Rational, yes, but a sinner whose rationality has been twisted by their sin.]
2. By publishing the law and punishing the law-breaker, man will, in self-interest, refrain from breaking the law [*general deterrence*].

49

3. We are entitled to punish you because your act against self-interest displayed your *mens rea*:

> **Mens rea (menz-a).** [Law Latin *"guilty mind"*] (1861) The state of mind that the prosecutor, to secure a conviction, must prove that a defendant had when committing a crime; criminal intent or recklessness <the *mens rea* for theft is the intent to deprive the rightful owner of the property>. *Mens rrea* is the second of the two essential elements of every crime at common law, the other being the *actus rea.* – Also termed *mental elements; criminal intent; guilty mind.*

The source for the theology/philosophy was found in passages such as:

> **Deuteronomy 6:1-3** Now this is the instruction, the laws, and the precepts which the Lord your God commanded me to teach you, that you might do them in the land to which you to possess it. That you may [reverently] **fear** the Lord your God, you and your son and your son's son, and keep all His statutes and His commandments which I command you all the days of your life, and that your days may be prolonged. Hear therefore, O Israel, and be watchful to do them, that it may be well with you and that you may increase exceedingly, as the Lord, the God of your fathers, has promised you, in a land flowing with milk and honey.

I would agree with the first of the three theological propositions about law but for the fact that our rationally is warped by our sin. To the extent our conflicts arises from our sin, our rationality self-destructs into spiritual blindness, a willingness to deny all and fight to the death in the courts to be justified.

In addition, there is no empirical proof for General Deterrence. There is some support for the proposition that punishing John may deter John from his specific bad act in the future, but not necessarily a different type of future bad act – a doctrine known as *special deterrence*.

Mens rea is not a part of God's *torah* — except possibly for what we call Pre-meditated, First-Degree, Murder – for he does not want us to play a game with our deceptively wicked heart and darkened mind, as that will only lead to self-imprisonment.

However, and most importantly for our consideration, the use of the English word, *fear,* in this passage is, in my opinion, a twist of Satan, and stands in opposition to the Deuteronomy 6:1-3 passage.

It is absolutely true that God gives us His Word "written on our hearts" [Deuteronomy 30:9-20], and that, as we come to know it and understand it and choose to in love for Him act out His Words, our "lives are prolonged", and things "go well with us." But that does not arise from a *terror* of God, but rather from a *reverential attitude towards* God.

Terror keeps us buried in the bushes.

This brings me to another translation issue. The Hebrew word translated as **fear** in this passage is *yare'. Strong's* [H3373] says this:

> A prime root; to fear; **morally** to revere. To frighten; affright; be (make) afraid, dread(-ful), (put in) fear (-ful, -fully, -ing), be had in) **reverence**(-end), [idiom] see, terrible (act, -ness, thing).

Vine's adds this:

> Used of a person in exalted position, *yare'* connotes "standing in awe." This is not simple fear, but reverence, whereby an individual recognizes the power and position of the individual revered and renders him proper respect. In this sense, the word may imply submission to a proper ethical relationship to God

God is certainly of an "exalted position"!

Thus the creators of the *Amplified Topical Reference Bible* [Zondervan, 1987] introduce the Book of Deuteronomy with the following comments:

> "Deuteronomy" is derived from the Greek word *Deuteronomion,* meaning "second lawgiving," and is the name given to this book by the *Septuagint* (Greek Old Testament) translators.

In the addresses recorded in Deuteronomy, Moses summarizes the essence of Israel's religion. **"Not Law, but Covenant" is the basic idea in the relationship <u>initiated by God</u> with Israel**. … Genuine love for God would be evident in such a reverence and respect for God and commitment to Him that they would naturally be concerned with obeying the divine *instruction* pertaining to holy living. Consequently justice and righteousness would permeate their daily lives, as their love was extended to their fellow brothers and sisters. [My emphasis added throughout.]

Might I add: "and to the widow, orphan and stranger in the land as a witness to the Greatness and Goodness of God"?

I am sorry to say that there are actually 18 different Hebrew words which are each translated in a nuanced range from *terror* to *revere*. After many hours of finding the verses, I found I could make no sense for why any one word was used in any particular instance in a particular passage.

So let me put this into a case setting, and take us back to Adam and Eve.

I suggest that *terror* of God and their future prompted Adam and Eve to jump into the bushes.

Their pause to contemplate Him led them to *revere* Him, and they came out in trust. You have to make your own choice here, but please consider Romans 8:1, 8:15, and I John 4:18 as you do so.

Consider also the following question: Of Whom is the author of Psalm 119 (The Psalm of the Law) writing — a God of a punitive nature just itching to zap us, or a God giving loving instructions (grain) to His lost sheep?

May *reverence* for God motivate your decision to choose His path to walk when you are in any form of conflict.

Allow me to take a few more words on the question of: "On what *basis* do we decide if a particular person should be punished for a particular act?"

The first part of the answer to the dilemma of our fathers in the secular law was the adoption of the doctrine of *Fault*:

fault. (13c) **1.** An error or defect in judgment or of conduct; any deviation from prudence or duty resulting from inattention, incapacity, perversity, bad faith, or mismanagement. See NEGLIGENCE. Cf. LIABILITY, **2.** *Civil Law.* The intentional or negligent failure to maintain some standard of conduct when that failure results in harm to another person. [*Black's.*]

Fault became: (a) *Intent* (a knowing and intentional act); *Recklessness* (acting while knowing of a high potential for causing harm, and a heedless disregard of that possibility); (c) *Negligence* (doing, or failing to do some thing a reasonable and prudent person would do or not do, when you have a duty to others to do or not do the act).

Please notice the mind-reading aspect of all of this.

Please notice that if no duty has been declared, you may get away with the whole thing – albeit God still knows, and so do you.

Of the mind, God says it: can vacillate (have two minds); change; plot evil; be made dull; be blinded; be closed; troubled; disturbed; anxious; doubting, and, only God can know it. [Jeremiah 20:12; in the list from the *Amplified* Topical Index.]

God says our un-regenerated hearts are: proud; foolish; deceitful; rebellious; perverse; evil; wicked; callous; malicious; hardened; darkened; deluded' unrepentant; unbelieving; gone astray; devoted to idols; filled with schemes to do wrong; filled with madness; far from God, and, "deceitful above all things." [Jeremiah 17:9; in the lists from the *Amplified* Topical Index.]

In short, God does not want us playing games with our mind or heart when in a conflict!

The second part of the answer to their dilemma (the inability to read the mind) was the adoption of a presumption: "The doing of an act establishes the intent to do the act."

This allows us to distinguish Tom from John when both punch someone in the nose and one pleads temporary insanity and sells that story to the jury, while the other is convicted of a crime.

And it separates both of them for the one who strikes in a reflex action, like when the doctor hits your elbow and your arm shoots out and hits his nurse and breaks your hand. Your act is without *legal fault* at all!

Yet both doctor and patient may be found liable for money damages (doctor to you for your hand and doctor to nurse for allowing her to be too close) in our law of Torts for being negligent. And the doctor could, for this single act, be charged as a criminal <u>and as</u> a tort-feasor and punished twice — <u>with total constitutionality</u> for the crime offended the State while the tort offended the patient and nurse.

In my opinion, it is these secular philosophies – *publish the law, punish for fault, to deter evil* — which are at the root of every complaint we have about our legal system, a system all seem to agree is broken. Our complaints have even brought the Koch brothers, Hillary Clinton and Rand Paul into common cause – miracle of miracles, but I digress.

It is also my opinion that *punish for fault to deter evil* is not supported by Scripture. However, this is not the place to fully flesh that out. I am working on another book: *Toward a Biblical View of "Criminal" "Justice"*, which will expand on our legal history, philosophy and methodology, and include a set of proposals for changes to our Criminal Justice systems so that those coming into the system might have a better opportunity to experience God's *peace* and *justice* by walking His path.

Now allow me to set yet one more proposition in place: What we ended up with post-William the Conqueror were two systems <u>competing for handling the conflicts of the people</u> — State and Church. What that produced can be summarized as follows:

<u>CHURCH</u>	<u>STATE</u>
Law from God	Law from King/State
Mediated through the Church	Mediated through the
King's courts	
Confessional Booth	Right to remain silent
Penance to the Church	Fines to the State
Inquisition/purgatory	Imprisonment
Excommunication	Execution

In short, they each produced a punitive model.

If you doubt this, check your Bible and see if you have "Church Discipline" interlineated between Matthew 18, verses 14 and 15. Yet Matthew 18:12-14 is a story of rescuing a stray sheep! How then do we get to disciplining/punishing someone – unless we are in tears when we do it

I will return to this question later.

God's Instructions: Purpose, Method & Blessings

Applying the philosophers' adage — Source determines Purpose, which determines Method, which produces Consequences — and having looked briefly at the purpose, method and consequences from Man's criminal law system, let's consider God's purpose and method.

The Source of Law: Obviously, God.

The Purpose of His Word:

> **Romans 3:19-20.** Now we know that whatever the Law says, it speaks to those who are under the Law, so that [the murmurs and excuses] of every mouth may be hushed and all the world may be held accountable to God. For no person will be justified (made righteous, acquitted, and judged acceptable) in His sight by the Law. For [the real function of] the Law is to make men recognize *and* be conscious of sin [not mere perception, but an acquaintance with sin which works towards repentance, faith and holy character].

> **Psalm 119:1.** BLESSED (HAPPY, fortunate, to be envied) are the undefiled (the upright, truly sincere, and blameless) in the way [of the revealed will of God], who walk (order their conduct and conversation) in the law of the Lord (the whole of God's revealed will).

His purposes and Word include all of the following things:

Psalm 119:2 – His testimonies
Psalm 119:3 – His precepts and ways

Psalm 119:5 – His promises

Psalm 119:7 – I will praise and give thanks to You when I learn [by sanctified experiences] Your righteous judgments [Your decisions against and punishments for particular thought and conduct].

Psalm 119:11– His Word we put into our hearts to conform our life to His

Psalm 119:15 – He marks out our paths of life

Psalm 119:24 – His testimonies are my delights and counselors

Psalm 119:39 – His ordinances are good

Psalm 119:40 – His precepts give me renewed life

Psalm 119:42 – they are an answer for those who taunt *and* reproach me, and something I can lean on, rely on, and trust in

Psalm 119:43 – we can hope in His ordinances

Psalm 119:45 – we can walk in liberty and at ease in Your precepts

Psalm 119:46 – we can speak of His testimonies also before kings and not be put to shame

Psalm 119:50 – Your word has revived me and given me life

Need I go further?

But you should read the rest of the Psalm, and ponder upon His goodness in giving us His *torah*.

His Method (when we are dealing with conflicts, and seeking *Justice*):

If men contend with each other, and a pregnant woman [interfering] is hurt so that she has a miscarriage, yet no further damage follow [the one who hurt her] shall surely be punished with a fine [paid] to the woman's husband, as much as the judges determine. But if any damage follows, then you shall give life for life, eye for eye [etc]. [Ex. 21:22-23.]

According to my Hebrew scholar friend, the concept here is actually that the one who struck shall pay as the husband demands, and if not, as the judge may declare, meaning you cannot go to the judge without trying to work things out between you, with help of the community as necessary. [See Matthew 5:20-26; Matthew 18:12-20; and I Corinthian 6:1-8]. The message is the same in all: first try to work things out!

The Jews had a *Bet Din*, a court-like system in each Synagogue to help with the squabbles of daily life.

However, people have reminded me of Exodus 22:5-6, and say it stands for our legal propositions of negligence, recklessness, or liability for inherently dangerous activity. So let us look at the passage:

> 5. If a man causes a field or vineyard to be grazed over or lets his beast loose and it feeds in another man's filed, he shall make restitution of the best of his own field or his own vineyard. If a fire breaks out and catches so that the stacked grain or standing grain or the field be consumed, he who kindled the fire shall make restitution.

Here we think we see negligence, recklessness, or inherently dangerous activity which fits into our *fault* concept. But those ideas are not in the verses; the verses show what we call *strict liability*:

> **Strict liability.** (1844) Liability that does not depend on actual negligence or intent to harm, but that is based on the breach of an absolute duty to make something safe. Strict liability most often applies either to ultrahazardous activities or in products-liability cases. – Also termed *absolute liability; liability without fault.* Cf. *Fault liability*; OUTCOME RESPONSIBILITY. [*Black's*].

I can tell you from my analysis that all of God's *Instructions* are based on "responsibility for an act done from which a harm results." God has a very *good purpose* for that approach. But before looking at it, let's look at the fire case — which I may see differently, having once started a brush fire that escaped:

> We checked and the weather was going to be calm. We had four of us to "work the borders". We had buckets of water, and tarps for beating down a fire. We notified the local

fire department and got their blessing to proceed. Then a sudden great wind blew in, and the fire started racing uphill towards my neighbor's house. We stopped it, but I thought I was going to die from the exertion.

But if the fire had continued escaping, and burned my neighbor's house, I had a number of defenses:

1. I was not *negligent*, for I took all the protective steps which a *reasonably prudent man* [RPM] *would take*, and since I was acting as a RPM should act, there is no negligence.
2. If you charge me with doing an inherently dangerous act, I am still not liable for the great, sudden and totally unpredicted wind was an *Act of God* which relieves me from liability at law!

Under Man's law, I have lots of rights and defenses to any charge of negligent or reckless behavior in this situation, but from God's strict liability approach, I have none.

You see, He knows "stuff" is going to happen, and does not want us to play the blame or excuse game with our hearts and mind. Instead, He wants us to see our responsibility to live in "a community awareness" of my neighbor at all times, and make amends for the acts I do which cause a harm.

What God wants is for us to work these things out, with the help of friends and neighbors as necessary [Exodus 21:22-23; Matthew 18:12-20]. He does not want us running to the courts [I Corinthians 6:7-8; Matthew 5:25-26], or other secular "helps".

Why not go to the secular systems?

> For three proofs that *relationship* is a big deal with God, consider: three-in-one yet one; husband and wife become one-flesh; the Body of Christ, consisting of millions of pieces each doing as led by the Spirit under a single Head (Christ), yet in unity.

Why go to one another, with the help of others?

Ephesians 4:30-32: ... [t]o not grieve the Holy Spirit of God [do not offend or vex or sadden Him], by Whom you were sealed (marked, branded as God's own, secured) for the day of redemption (of final deliverance through Christ from evil and the consequences of sin). Let all bitterness and indignation *and* wrath (passion, rage, bad temper) and resentment (anger, animosity) and quarreling (brawling, clamor, contention) and slander (evil-speaking, abusive or blasphemous language) be banished from you, with all malice (spite, ill will, or baseness of any kind). And become useful *and* helpful *and* kind to one another, tenderhearted (compassionate, understanding, loving-hearted), forgiving one another [readily and freely] as God in Christ forgave you."

Why not go to the courts?

Galatians 5:15: But if you bite and devour one another [in partisan strife], be careful that you [and your whole fellowship] are not consumed by one another."

Why go to one another to seek help?

Hebrews 12:15: Exercise foresight *and* be on the watch to look [after one another], to see that no one falls back from *and* fails to secure God's grace (His unmerited favor and spiritual blessing), in order that no root of resentment (rancor, bitterness, or hatred) shoots forth and causes trouble *and* bitter torment, and many become contaminated *and* defiled by it.

As believers in God's Christ, why work things out?

John 17:21: That we may all may be one, [just] as You, Father, are in Me and I in You, that we also may be one in Us, so that the world may believe *and* be convinced that You have sent Me."

<u>Why not go to the courts?</u>

> Romans 12:18: So that we might be restored in our
> relationship with the One Who Created us, provides for
> us, sustains us — and restored with our fellow Believers,
> and with one another, "and, if possible, as far as it depends
> on you, live at peace with everyone."

Our legal system cares nothing about the things of God. Its job is to make a decision because you have forced it to do by coming to it.

Its only tool is a sword, and it will wield it and cut things apart in the process – which is also why *gossip* and *tale-bearing* are in God's list of sins, for it divides people. [*see*, Romans 1:28-32; but I digress.]

Let's look at Solomon for a moment, the wisest man ever [I Kings 3:5-28]:

Do you think God told Solomon that if he threatened to cut the baby in half the true mother would be disclosed, and Solomon would be able to recognize her as the true mother?

I don't; I've been there and done that in divorce and juvenile court. I did it because the law and the people standing before me left me no choice, having refused to work things out between them with the help of others.

I also believe Solomon knew that the people of his kingdom were divided as to who should get the child, and that division would continue after his decision and affect his ability forever to be seen as a good king. Thus he may have thought that if he divided the child, the people of his kingdom might be united, albeit in anger at him, but at least united.

We don't know. But we see the results of God honoring the actions of a man dedicated to serve Him in his official role as a judge. I also saw such a thing take place in open court because I chose to speak truth, and not law into a divorce conflict:

> The husband and wife, both represented by attorneys,
> stood before me for a hearing to determine who should
> live in the house while the divorce case worked its way
> through the court.
>
> The husband was on the witness stand saying he wanted to
> because, with $25,000 and his labor he could complete the

house he had been building by hand above the basement where he lived with his wife and three kids, and gain at least $50,000 in the process.

I interrupted the questioning to ask him if he was aware that his wife hated that house; she would live with him in a mud hut if he was ever home, but he was either at work or building the house and collapsing from lack of sleep.

Ooops! I apologized for injecting that, and ordered it stricken from the record.

Later the wife was testifying, and I broke in to tell her that I thought I understood her husband: he, like me was of German background, and if he were standing in front of St. Peter asking for admission to Heaven, and Peter asked, "Why", the man would say, "because I loved my family", and point to the house as proof of that love.

Ooops! I apologized again, and called a 10-minute break to collect my emotions.

I came back out, and only the attorneys were there; their clients had left to find a counselor because they realized they did not know each other.

A week later they came back, without their attorneys, and asked me to dismiss their case, for they had reconciled. I was BLESSED, HAPPY to do so.

What I did was not judicious; it was out of bounds. But what would a system look like if it were allowed?

When we put all this together with Prov. 29:26, and Micah 6:8, we should be able to agree with God that *Justice* – whatever it may be – will never be known by us through a study and practice of man's laws and methods.

Nor will it come to us through our courts, for what comes through our courts is in the form of a blindfolded lady, carrying a law book and wielding a sword, who has no choice but to cut and divide those who will not practice God's way to deal with their conflicts but chose to ignore His *torah* and war against one another.

These things also show that a choice of going to the Law when in conflict, more often than not produces a *consequence* of embittering the souls of the participants, leaving them angry, confused, and crying out for *justice*. [I Cor. 6:7-8; Matt. 5:25-26.]

In contrast, there are many stories in the Bible (and I have many from my years in the Ministry of Reconciliation) which show that if you walk God's *way* when in conflict – *a way* of *speaking truth, presenting peace, confessing harms caused, forgiving harms done* and *helping to bear the burdens caused by conflicts* – you will be able to survive the conflict without being permanently and irrevocably scarred by its process, and you can find peace as the conflict continues, as well as at its end.

And all of this is regardless of what the other party chooses to do or not do.

I write these thoughts having been a lawyer helping people war over their rights and property in the courts.

I write having been a judge adjudicating those wars, and swinging the sword and cutting those standing near.

I write as one who has walked the past 6.5 years in a nightmare in the courts of man; sometimes walking above it, and sometimes the mire sucked the life out of me.

Therefore, I can agree with our Lord and Savior: "There is no good thing waiting there in the courts." [Matt. 5:5:25, paraphrased.]

If you sense me crying while writing this, you are correct. It's also what I did most weekends when Judge – in anger and frustration. But my tears today are of joy.

Some Truths of Law-Words

As I continue in my exhortation for you to come first to the Body of Christ when in need of help with a conflict, allow me to tell you something else about the differences between Man's *law-words* and God's *Instruction-words*.

Our *Law-words* are not like words of medicine, carpentry, mathematics and the like. Such words can be translated with ease into the language of another country, for they are firm, and detached from history and philosophy.

In contrast, *Law-words* carry with them a *peculiar history*, a *peculiar philosophy* (a/k/a *theology* according to Rushdoony), and a *peculiar methodology* unique to the time and place in which they arose and where they are practiced. As such, law-words lack precision; they can change over time and literally "black" can come to mean "white".

> I discovered while in Moscow that the people of Kazakhstan, where I was to later go and teach, did not have "written words of law" in their language; only in Russian. They had never bothered because they had an oral tradition for how to deal with conflict, and thus needed no written *law-words*! Amazing!

Furthermore, law-words are not *self-actuating.* You might even go so far as to say they have no meaning at all until two people are in a conflict. Then they want to know what the words mean, and the impact of them on the outcome of the conflict.

One lawyer says the black dots on the paper mean ABC, while the other says MNO. Both clients then pay large sums of money to their lawyers, only to get to hear a judge say that they actually mean XYZ!

Today, in the United States, there is little certainty in the law because it lacks any internal sense of absolutes due to the changeability of the meaning of the *law-words*.

And in our system, if you change a single material fact in a dispute you may well change the *law- words* which will control the outcome, and thereby change the nature of the outcome, all the time being true to the law as a whole.

None of this means that the law system *does justice*, only that it produces *a law-decision*. That *law-system* and its *law-decision* are ruled over by fallible people, so any unforced error, let alone a forced error of a judge, can produce a massive *injustice*.

Because of these realities, the law says that a judge may, at any time and after no matter how long a time, rework a *law-decision* to avoid a *manifest injustice*. As you might imagine, hen's teeth are more common than such reversals by judges. As I said, I expect to write on this aspect of the law in the near future.

But is such a fluid system where you want to go when in conflict?

Some Truths of God's Word

God, on the other hand, says of Himself:

> For I am the Lord. I do not change; that is why you, O sons of Jacob, are not consumed. [Malachi 3:6.]

Consumed? Oh Lord, what do you mean here? Is it that without the rock of your gracious instructions we are unmoored from all things, and the world will chew us up and spit us out?

God also says that His *words* are:

> not too difficult for you;

> not far off;

> not a [secret laid up] in heaven, that you should say, Who shall go up for us to heaven and bring it to us, that we may hear and do it?

> neither is it beyond the sea, that you should say, Who shall go over the sea for us and bring it to us that we may hear and do it?

> but the word is very near you, in your mouth and in your mind *and* in your heart [WDB: the *Imago Dei* in which we are made?], so that you can do it.

> See, I have set before you this day life and good, and death and evil [WDB: as consequences of willingness or unwillingness to follow the *words*?]. [Deuteronomy 30:11-15.]

As I said to my students in the former U.S.S.R.: "You have heard from me words about the *laws* and *ways* of man, and the *instructions* and *ways* of God. As you grow, and live, and seek to engage in adopting words and methods for your laws and legal systems, as well as for your personal life-style, please choose carefully, and always consider the *instructions* of the Lord."

What follows are a number of other things which I taught them, things which bear on my thesis about our Image of God.

Defining Law:

My first day of each semester with my students began with a set of questions:

What is law?

Where do we find law?

Where do we encounter law in action?

Where do our laws come from?

How does law operate.

What do we want from our laws; i.e. why do we have law

Black's starts with this:

> **law.** (bef. 12c) **1.** The regime that orders human activities and relations **through systematic application of the force** of politically organized society, or through **social pressure, backed by force**, in such a society; the legal system <respect and obey the law>. **2.** The aggregate of legislation, judicial precedents, and accepted legal principles; the body of authoritative grounds of judicial and administrative action; esp., the body of rules, standards, and principles that the courts of a particular jurisdiction apply in deciding controversies brought before them <the law of the land>. **3.** The set of rules or principles dealing with a specific area of a legal system <copyright law>. **4.** The judicial and administrative process; legal action and proceedings <when settlement negotiation failed, they submitted their dispute to the law>. **5.** A statute <Congress

passed a law>. – Abbr. L. **6.** COMMON LAW <law but not equity>. **7.** The legal profession <she spent her entire career in the law>. [*Black's;* Emphasis added.]

Please note that we are, early on, brought to accept the proposition that, without power to back it up, *law*, if it exists at all, is meaningless for those who decide to pay it no mind — i.e., *deterrence* is a false doctrine. And that is true not only as to the anarchist, but also the one who merely does not know that the law has something to say on what they are doing, i.e., "ignorance of the law is no excuse".

Where do we find Law?

It starts in our homes as we grow up. Then we find it in our schools, on our streets, and in our shops, factories, and voluntary societies. It is in every branch of Government.

And in each and every instance it may be written or unwritten, active or passive — but it is always "there".

Where does law come from?

Ultimately, there are <u>only</u> two possible sources for man:

A. The "mind of man", having, we hope, rationally (albeit rationality darkened by The Fall), from consideration of all accumulated knowledge — wisely choosing our options. But if that were <u>always</u> true, how did Hitler become *Hitler*?

B. A pre-existing, ever valid in every situation, applicable to every person who has ever lived or will ever live, *Law* from outside of man, which – praise to its Author – has graciously been made known to man, and which will vindicate Itself before man in all of its righteousness and justice.

If there is only the first of these two, then there are no absolutes; all is situational ethics, and there are no rules for the ball-game of life — so go for the gusto! [a beer slogan in the '60's].

I was invited to sit and interact with what I thought was going to be a small group of law students in Brest, Belarus.

> At 1:00 AM on the day of the gathering, as I was being shown to my room in a former KGB Hotel for the rest of the night, I was told that I was going to be the plenary speaker at: (a) a conference on Human Rights; (b) on International Human Rights Day; (c) on the 3rd anniversary of the President of Belarus having thrown out the courts and parliament and converted himself into a classical Soviet Strongman; (d) in a city noted for being a hotbed of resistance; and (e) shortly after I discovered that President Lukashenko had declared me to be "an example of modern Western Imperialism" on the 5 national television stations.
>
> I was not a happy camper
>
> As I undressed, I silently cried out: "Lord, I don't talk about human rights; that is not smart under the circumstances in which I teach. HELP!"
>
> A single sentence-thought came to my mind, and I went peacefully to sleep, awaking with about a 15-minute presentation framed out in my mind. My late-night initial thought was this:
>
> If we are all evolved from a primordial sludge-pot, it is arrogant and futile to say we have *rights*. Human rights only exist if there is a Creator, who creates us – unique and distinct from the rest of His creation. And, then, it is not our *rights* which we need to seek to understand, but our *responsibilities* to our Creator *vis-a-vis* Him and all of His creation.

At 9:00 am I went on to flesh that out relative to living in the legal/political environment of the day in Belarus. I made the presentation, took questions for an hour – and went on to finish out the semester without being arrested.

You see, the laws of man operate almost exclusively in reaction to some one's actions or inactions. That is part of the reason why there is no statistical proof of our theory of *general deterrence.*

It is also because law is not self-actuating, and I have to choose to allow it to govern me; that is actually the best understanding of *Rule-of- Law;* i.e., not that law rules us by compulsion, but that we submit to the law as something of value.

Finally, if I do not submit to the law, consequences **will** flow upon me, **but only if I am caught and cannot beat the system**.

God's *instructions* are dramatically different.

First, His *instructions* for Life are *Truth-statements* because He is *Truth.*

Second, *consequences* **do and will flow** from our choices, even if I am not caught by man. My effort to hide my sin from the world will store up bad things within me and affect those around me. [See: Joshua 7:1-13; Hebrews 12:15.]

Third, God's *instructions* **promise** I can have peace in the midst of conflict/turmoil **when I follow Him**, and I can walk free of shame and guilt because I strive to follow them; i.e., I am not paralyzed by the past. [Romans 8:1.]

These do not mean I do not have to deal with consequences from my prior wrong actions, nor does it mean that something measurable as "good" (health, wealth, whatever) will flow to me by obedience, or that no bad thing will descend upon me. It just means I can sleep like a baby at night because I have God's *Justice*, and can trust my future to Him.

What do we want from our Laws?

When I came to this question, the students startled me. They all started with "order" as the purpose for law, i.e., a peaceful environment to live in, rather than being assaulted by. But they also said they wanted the law <u>to help them with their conflicts</u>. Amazing!

You see, man's law can give you a place to go to with a conflict so you avoid having the conflict turn into a 30-year Hatfield and McCoy feud — and it is good to have a place to go.

But Law does not help you **resolve** the conflict, it **adjudicates** it and parcels out **consequences** – which you accept or reject at your peril.

As I pressed the students to develop this expression of their desire for help, what I found was they knew that the law of their nation had nothing for them if they went to it seeking something. That is very typical of law under a totalitarian, for the purpose of that law is to keep the totalitarian in power, and you out of his hair.

And yet, while they acted in terms of a lack of fairness in the law, they still believed that the law and legal system **could**, in fact, **help** them when in need! They saw it as a source of *justice* even though all of their past showed it as only *unjust*.

It is amazing how we can delude ourselves!

Defining Justice:

Sir John Fortescue attempted to interest the young prince in reading the book by saying that *justice* came through the Law of England.

But *righteousness* and *justice* are two of the foundations of the throne of God. [Psalm 89:14.]

I told my students that they should be interested in *Justice*, and for that topic I would look to my Bible. I invited them to bring their holy books, and even their religious leaders for those discussions; sadly, none ever did that. But they were very, very interested in *Justice* as a subject for discussion.

A short aside is in order here.

> In my first year in Moscow [1994], I had a chance to meet with a group of 5th year philosophy students. I began by asking them what they had learned in their Philosophy of Law class. They said they did not have that class. "Oh, so it is in your last semester?" "No; we do not have such a class."
>
> Dumb me; of course you cannot philosophize about law in a totalitarian system unless you can couch it in nothing but hypothetical terms — and it is impossible to philosophize about law in a vacuum, for you have to present factual conflicts to which you apply your philosophy to show how great it is!

Their first and most common response to the question of "What is Justice" was: *fairness*. This is a universally recognized synonym. For example, *Wikipedia* defines *justice* as: "the legal or philosophical **theory** by which fairness is *administered*." Note this is presented as a statement of a *theory*, and not *truth-fact*, and it focuses on *process* and not *outcome*, but presumes the *outcome* to be just because the *process* was just.

Circuitous reasoning writ large!

Our inherent problem here is that *fairness* is a word which always, and only flows from a comparison of one situation with another. But every time you change a single material fact in a case at law, you have a high potential of changing the outcome; so you are left with little for true comparison when comparing cases to discover fairness, a/k/a *justice*.

This problem with defining *Justice* can also be shown by reference to *Black's*, knowing that *jus* meant "law, right" in Latin, and:

> ***Jus:*** ... the entire body of **principles**, **rules**, and **statutes**, whether written or unwritten, by which the public and the private *rights*, the *duties* and the *obligations* of men, as members of a community, are **defined**, **inculcated**, **protected** and **enforced**. William Ramsey, *A Manual of Roman Antiquities* 285-86 (Rudolfo Lanciana ed., 15th ed., 1894) [*Black's*, pg 936.]

This is Fortescue's idea: "flowing from our rules and processes."

But can you see the truth of Rushdooney that religion and law are in a direct head- on collision over declaring what is or is not just, and for dealing with the conflicts of the people? Can you see that you can insert God's *torah* in place of *jus* at the beginning of the quote and the statement becomes a *Truth* statement as opposed to a lie?

In *Black's*, after seven pages of *jus* + another word, we come finally to *justice* itself:

> **justice.** (17v) **1.** The fair and proper administration of laws.
>
> [WDB: i.e., the <u>product</u> of a <u>process</u> is equated with a word; circuitous reasoning.]

2. A judge, esp. of an appellate court or a court of last resort.

> [WDB: A human being replaces God as source of *justice*.]

3. *Hist.* Judicial cognizance of causes or offenses; jurisdiction.

> [WDB: Here the <u>process</u> <u>itself</u> is equated with *justice*; also circuitous reasoning.]

Black's then goes on with 11 more definitions – and a 12th if you know where to look:

> **commutative justice** (1856) Justice concerned with the relations between persons and esp. with <u>fairness</u> in the exchange of goods and fulfillment of contractual obligations.
>
> > [WDB: As determined by whom, if they cannot determine by themselves?]
>
> **condign justice** An outcome according to what the litigants <u>deserve</u>; esp. justice based on the kind and degree of punishment that is appropriate for a given offense.
>
> > [WDB: Deserve? Under what standard? Our legislatures decree punishment by mandating sentences based on the nature of the offense and past actions of the offender, plotted out on a grid – all without ever meeting a single offender or their victim. Is that *just*? I sent a 26-year old to prison for 32-years for 3 petty crimes over a span of 8-years with a total "loss" of $25.00 to individuals.]

distributive justice (16c) Justice <u>owed by</u> a community to its members, including the fair allocation of common advantages and sharing of common burdens.

> [WDB: As determined by whom or by what standard? Does not this presume that a "group" can actually *do justice*?]

Jedburgh justice A brand of justice involving punishment (esp. execution) first and trial afterwards. The term alludes to Jedburgh, a Scottish border town where in the 17th century raiders were said to have been hanged without the formality of a trial. Jedburgh justice differs from lynch law in that the former was administered by an established court (albeit after the fact).

> [WDB: I imagine the one lynched said, "UNJUST!"]

natural justice Justice as defined in a *moral*, as opposed to *legal* sense. Also termed *justitia naturalis*.Cf. NATURAL LAW.

> [WDB: a loose term which allows a court to correct a decision when a party has been deprived of an opportunity to present his or her side of the case.]

personal justice. (16c) Justice between parties to a dispute, regardless of any <u>larger principles</u> that might be involved. – Also termed *justice in personam; popular justice; social justice*.

> [WDB: What, pray tell, are those "larger principles"? So Joe and John get *justice* in their squabble, and the whole community suffers? Is that someone's concept of *just*?]

Popular justice. (17c) Demotic justice, which is usu. considered less than fully fair and proper even though it satisfies prevailing public opinion in a particular case. Cf. *Social justice*. "Nothing is more treacherous than popular justice in many of its manifestations, subject as it is to passion, to fallacy, and to the inability to grasp general notions, or to distinguish the essential from the inessential." Carleton K. Allen, *Law in the Making*, 387 (7th ed. 1964).

> [WDB: Are you kidding me with this twisted language? So now the community gets *justice*, but Joe and John do not?]

Positive justice. (17c) Justice as it is conceived, recognized, and *incompletely expressed by* the civil law or some other form of *human law*. Cf. Positive law.

> [WDB: If a judgment is "incompletely expressed" under the civil law, how can it ever be called *valid*, let alone *just*?]

preventative justice. Justice intended to protect against a future misbehavior. Specific types of preventative justice include appointing a receiver or administrator, issuing a restraining order or injunction, and binding over to keep the peace.

> [WDB: No law, nor system, nor court order can ever protect anyone from anything when another decides to not be bound by the order.]

social justice. (1902) **1.** Justice that conforms to a moral principle, such as that all people are equal. **2.** One or more equitable resolutions sought on behalf of individuals and communities who are disenfranchised, under-represented, or otherwise excluded from meaningful participation in legal, economic, cultural, and social structure, with the ultimate goal of removing barriers to participation and effecting social change. – Also termed *justice in rem* [i.e., "in a thing of property]. Cf. *Personal justice*; *cause lawyering*

[WDB: I see *social justice* as something for the Body of Christ to be to one-another and to the world, not a thing which can flow from government. For more on this, I would refer you to pages 148-169, *Generous Justice*, by Timothy Keller, (Dutton, 2010).

[Today we also have *environmental justice*, which *Wikipedia* defines as: "the fair treatment and meaningful involvement of all people regardless of race, color, national origin, or income with respect to the development, implementation, and enforcement of environmental laws, regulations, and policies." It is thus aimed at giving seats at the table to those who were or will be, because of social status, unable to prevent their being harmed by the disregard for the environment by nation or entity, when consideration is being given to initial development or correcting damaging development. That they be given a seat at the table is absolutely *just*; that the result of the table's actions will be *justice* is false; it will be law.]

Substantial justice. (17c) Justice fairly administered according to the rules of substantive law, regardless of any procedural errors not affecting the litigant's substantive rights; a fair trial on the merits.

[WDB: Are you comfortable with the idea that something may be declared *just* even though there have been procedural errors, simply by a Judge saying that the errors did not affect *substantive rights*? [*Black's*: "A right that can be enforced by law; a right of substance rather than form."]

Before going to the 12th definition, I want you to consider that, in every one of the 11 definitions above, there is the inherent idea that someone is looking at a case from the outside, and making a judgment as to whether or not justice was done. Phrased differently, a judge has made a judgment, and that judgment is now being examined externally as to its *fairness* or *justice* by an outsider to the case.

At least the Judge heard all of the testimony, saw the exhibits, heard arguments and read case citations; not so the commentator.

Where, in all of these definitions are the voices of the participants themselves?

Do they see themselves as victims of a process run amok, now crying "UNJUST" over what has taken place, or are they smirking for having beaten the system?

And so I come to the 12th definition – which is not on the same pages as all the rest [*Black's* pgs 942-943], but on page 1428; why I do not know:

> **restorative justice** An alternative in delinquency **sanctions** focused on repairing the harm done, meeting the victim's needs, and holding the offender responsible for his or her actions. Restorative justice sanctions use a balanced approach, producing the least restrictive disposition while stressing the offender's accountability and providing relief to the victim. The offender may be ordered to make restitution, to perform community service, or to make amends in some other way that the court orders.

> [WDB: Note the use of **sanctions**. Note also that this definition does not describe the process. The *process* is that one who sees themself as a victim, and one who is accused of being an offender" [I use the words in the broadest of all possible senses], are brought together before "others" to try to talk through the events and find a common ground for going forward, while leaving bitterness behind.

> [*Wikipedia* has an excellent article, and multiple resources, on this topic, and it is worth the reader's review. There you will find references to Victim- Offender Reconciliation

[VORP], and the names of Howard Zehr, Ron Claassen, and Mark Umbreit, all of whom were there as we birthed VORP into the U.S. when I was the judge of the Elkhart Superior Court II, in Elkhart, Indiana. You will also find the name of Dan Van Ness – a friend of mine from my involvement with Chuck Colson and the Prison Fellowship Ministries. It was my introduction to VORP, and seeing the results of its use, which was to play such a major role in many of my future life choices, and in changing my image of God.]

In 1992, after nearly 10-years of trying to help people in conflict be reconciled to God and one another, and being confused by what I was encountering with the organized church, I took the time to look up every scripture in which *justice* or *righteousness* was found in the Bible. That is what led to the pamphlet, *Redefining and Rediscovering Justice*. [*see at* www.shepherdsforpeace.com]

In the process of that study, I also studied every passage in the New Testament where the Greek word, *poieo* [*make*; *Vine's* @ 386; *Strong's* #4160] appeared, for I had been troubled by not seeing myself as actually *making peace*. Matthew 5:9 says:

> Blessed (enjoying enviable happiness, spiritually prosperous— possessing with life-joy and satisfaction in God's favor and salvation, regardless of their outward conditions) are the *makers and* sustainers of peace, for they shall be called the sons of God.

In my analysis, I discovered two things:

a) *poieo* was also translated as: Peace-bearer; Peace-bringer; Peace-commiter; Peace-doer (did; does; done: doing); Peace-giver; Peace-offeror; Peace-performer; Peace-practicer; Peace-shower; Peace-treater – all situations wherein one does not cause a reaction but merely acts; and,

b) in every instance where I found a change taking place <u>within a person</u>, the *acting-agent* was God, Christ, the Spirit, or the Word.

That study brought me peace; i.e., I can do what I can do, but the outcome is for God. I can present peace and write on peace and model peace, but the listener/reader/watcher will have to choose to follow God's path to find and walk in peace when in conflict.

But I can certify to you from experience that practicing God's Ways can bring you the peace of *Shadrack et al* [Daniel 3] when you know you have acted justly towards man and God, regardless of the outcome.

Jay E. Adams, in his book, *A Theology of Christian Counseling* (Zondervan; 1979), said the following about Justice in view of the one-another counseling role of Believers:

> [Pgs 51-53] One age-old theme, constantly heard in the counseling room in one form or another, is, "It isn't fair!" In a pair of psalms, easily remembered by the reversal of their numbers (Psalms 37 and 73), both David and Asaph admit to entertaining such thoughts. The theme of each Psalm is the justice of God in a seemingly unjust world where the godly suffer and the ungodly prosper. The final act of each is contrasted, plus the immediate advantages of the faithful in those things that are of eternal worth. Eternity is contrasted with time, etc. One fact dominates all: God is in control, and the seeming injustice of the situation is only apparent. The imbalances often experienced are only temporary. The picture is larger than it may seem. This is the theme of the entire Bible. Indeed, it is a principle theme of the Cross. The serpent bites the Savior's heel (apparently gaining an upper hand) only as his own head is being crushed beneath it (Genesis 3:15). By His death, Christ conquers death. It is ever so in a world where a good God reigns.
>
> ....
>
> As much as counselees would like to hear otherwise, God's justice does not always appear immediately. Injustice all too often prevails for a time. It is true that sinners sow seeds of their own destruction, but, as the psalmist says, for a time they flourish and spread themselves "like a

green bay tree." During that time the imbalance of the scales is not easy for us to take.

But that is what faith is all about; faith looks off to the future (Hebrews 11). It takes the long view in dependence upon God's Word. All God's people have had to learn this. Counselees cannot expect to be exempted. The desire to be exempted may be the problem of some. Therefore, counselors must be ready to use the exhortation of the 37th and 73rd Psalms in counseling. When a counselee says, "That isn't fair!" he must be made aware of the seriousness of his accusation; he is challenging the justice of God and faithfulness of His Word. Moreover, he is exhibiting a clear lack of faith.

God is just. The righteous will be cared for (they don't beg bread). Their ultimate blessing is assured, and God in His time and in His way will right the wrongs. There is no easy way for counselees to arrive at this stance; yet that is precisely the need of so many. Envy, resentment and revenge, mixed with self-pity, constitute the bitter ingredients of very many counseling sessions. Therefore, every counselor should arm himself with the basic facts, and a few crucial passages (I have tried to set forth both concisely here) about God's justice. He must warn and encourage. He warns about accusing God of injustice, and encourages the long view of faith.

Here my friend Jay takes the long view. However, I suggest that there is also a short view.

Adam and Eve, as they were escorted out of the Garden, did not know what the future held except it was not going to be as pleasant as originally planned. They had no idea of anything which they could do to right their wrong — and I can't think they had any idea of God's long term plan wrapped up in the few words: "bruise the foot and crush the head."

But I do suggest that they out walked in peace.

My buddies Shadrack *et al* knew God was God and would still be God, and that was enough to proceed without recrimination against their executioner as they walked in peace towards the fire.

I have just ended a 6.5-year personal nightmare in the courts, ending in my being effectively disbarred, disgraced and bankrupteded. I had no idea during those years what the future of what any of my multiple steps on my step by step journey would bring, nor of what the future would be at the end of the journey. Yet much of the time I walked in peace.

Well, the specific journey ended June 18th, 2018 — and I still have no idea of God's purpose for that journey, or what the future holds. But I walk on in His peace and justice, knowing He is, ever will be, and wins in the end. And that is sufficient for the day.

The Prime Purpose for God's Instructions

As I said above, the Source determines the Purpose, the Purpose the Method, and the Method produces Consequences.

The Christian Bible teaches that God knew, before He created the Universe and all that is in it, and before He created "man in His likeness", that man was going to reject the *Instruction* of God, and break the original linkage between God and man.

He knew *sin* would flood all mankind, and even the cosmos.

He knew that the *sin* within us, the seeking of self over the seeking of Him, would blind and deafen us to His *Truth* [see, II Cor. 5:15].

Yet He remains absolute *Truth*, truly knowing what is best for us.

Thus it was right, proper, gracious and merciful that He communicate with mankind concerning how to live at peace as a fallen person in a fallen world — and He chose to do so.

> **Therefore, every word of His *Word*, His *Instructions*, is, at its heart, a word aimed at restoration of the original planned relationship between man and God, and man and man.**
>
> **Thus His *Method* for dealing with conflict is designed to enhance the possibility of that restoration occurring, and our being at peace in the struggle.**
>
> **While our Legal systems create terror in the heart, and the one who did a harm shuts down the very confession which opens the inner self to freedom.**

During the pre-*sin* time in the Garden, there was, in fact, perfect peace and harmony in all things and beings. His *Instructions* at that time were but two:

> And God blessed them and said to them, Be fruitful, **multiply**, and **fill the earth and subdue it** [using all its

vast resources in the service of God and man]; and have dominion over the fish of the sea, the birds of the air, and over every living creature that moves upon the earth. [Gen. 1:28]

You may freely eat of every tree in the garden; But of the tree of the knowledge of good and evil *and* blessing and calamity you shall not eat, for in the day that you eat of it you shall surely die. [Genesis 2:16-17.]

Have you ever wondered about why only two instructions?

I suggest the first was because He was going to walk with them in the cool of the day, and answer all of their questions; they had no need at the beginning for more *instruction* then those which were given, for they would receive from Him when more was needed.

While we may not understand why the second limitation was given, we must agree that it was given to help preserve God's desired form of relationship with mankind; i.e., to keep direct, rather than indirect relationship in place.

The insertion of the Holy Spirit in the Believer, following the resection of Christ from the tomb, restored that direct relationship.

But because of the original fracture of God's original purpose in the Garden, the remainder of the Bible, except for the last two chapters of The Revelation to John, is nothing more than God giving us information and case-studies of His longing to restore that which had been intended, inviting us to return to Him when we stray, and showing us His *way* to find Him.

The last thing in the world which He wants is for us to run away from Him in terror.

I have already broached the idea that God's *instructions* are *purposed* for showing us how to live <u>at</u> peace <u>in</u> a world maddened by sin: "If possible, as far as depends on you, live at peace with everyone." [Romans 12:18.] Here are some of my additional conclusions.

First, God has made it clear that there are consequences for disregarding His *instructions* [Deuteronomy 30:15-19]:

See, I have set before you this day life and good, and death and evil.

[If you obey the commandments of the Lord your God which] I command you today, to love the Lord your God, to walk in His ways, and to keep His commandments and His statutes and His ordinances, then you shall live and multiply, as the Lord your God will bless you in the land into which you go to possess.

But if your [mind and] heart turn away and you will not hear, but are drawn away to worship other gods and serve them, I declare to you today that you shall surely perish, and you shall not live long in the land which you pass over the Jordan to enter and possess.

I call upon heaven and earth to witness this day against you that I have set before you life and death, the blessings and curses; therefore, choose life that you and your descendants may live

Second, God does not sit there watching like a hawk for our slightest misstep so that He can zap us; i.e., He is not, at His core, punitive in His nature as is our criminal justice system.

You shall put the mercy seat on the top of the ark, and in the ark you shall place the Testimony [the 10 Commandments] that I will give you. There I will meet with you and, from above the mercy seat, from between the two cherubim that are upon the ark of the Testimony, I will speak intimately with you of all which I will give you in commandment to the Israelites. [Exodus 25:16-22.]

Third, God's approach is to look at the *fact* that we did something which hurt another and not the *reason why* or *mental state* involved; i.e., His *way* is *no-fault* and not *fault*. [I allow for the possibility that *mental state* might be involved in premeditated first degree murder; but that could be a myth of my creation.]

Fourth, He wants us to agree with Him that the act which we did caused a harm, take ownership of our act to the other(s) involved, and do what we can to help make things right.

Fifth, once repentance has taken place in the heart, we can ask our self, in front of others: "Help me to discover why I did what I did, and change my ways."

Sixth, His system is designed to allow us to be quickly restored to Him and to one another. [I John 1:8-9.]

Seventh, He does not declare us *persona non gratis*, or *irredeemable*, nor does He have *prisons*. Consider, in light of that, our definition of a Criminal:

> **Criminal,** n. (17c) **1.** One who has been convicted of a criminal offense. **2.** One who has been convicted of a crime.
>
> [WDB: Do you see here a judgment "of the essential nature of the person", i.e., "because you did this one thing you are of the nature of a criminal"?]

Eighth, He literally allows us to wallow in the *prisons* of our minds and souls that we have made for ourselves by rejecting His *instructions*, just as He allows us to *choose* to spend eternity in darkness, separated from Him – a place and status which personifies Hell.

But if our view of His *instructions*, and His Essence have been skewed by our bringing our legal philosophies into His *instructions*, then *fear* will rule us when in conflict, and we will not practice His *Ways*. That is what John was saying earlier, and which bears repeating:

> There is no fear in love [dread does not exist], but full-grown (complete, perfect) love turns fear out of doors, *and* expels every trace of terror! For fear brings with it the thought of punishment, and [so] he who is afraid has not reached the full maturity of love [is not yet grown into love's complete perfection]. I John 4:18.

Praise God that He gave us *instructions* for how to work through our conflicts in: Proverbs 19:11; I Corinthians. 6:1-8; Matthew. 5:21-26; Matthew 18:12-20; and, James. 5:13-16.

In contrast to the methods set forth by Jesus, consider the story of Jethro, Father-in- Law of Moses, and a "Priest of Midian", which means Jethro's roots were in Abraham through his wife, Keturah [see Genesis 25:1-2].

> In Exodus 18, Jethro appears to have accepted the God of Moses as his own, and he gave a burnt offering sacrifice to God [Exodus 18:8-12]. The next day [Exodus 18:12-26], Jethro awoke to find "the people" – does that mean all 600,000 men? — standing there in pairs waiting to get to Moses with their conflicts [vs. 13]. Being astute, Jethro said the obvious to Moses: "You need helpers!", and proposed a *system* for dealing with the conflicts of the people.

> If we think of Jethro as a new believer, just "born again", then the question we should ask is whether he was speaking for God; i.e., are his suggestions God's *way*?

> According to Exodus 12:37, 600,000 men crossed the Red Sea with Moses. Allowing for women, children, and non-Jews, we likely had a total population of around 2 million; but let's just calculate the number of judges from the 600,000 men:

> 60,000 to head the 10's
> 12,000 to head the 50's
> 6,000 to head the 100's
> 600 to head the 1000's
> 78,600 Judges needed out of over a million adults.

Thus, Jethro called for *justice* itself, and its delivery, to be systematized instead of allowing it to flow directly from God to His people as they would listen to Him orate His heart into His verbal *instructions*, and then walk in them.

Question: before these men are appointed, imagine yourself at the back of the line waiting to get to Moses, standing there along with your adversary. At the end of the day [vs. 13], you are still there. So you go home, collect some quail for dinner, sleep soundly, gather some manna in the morning, and get back in line.

How long will you do this until you look at your fellow citizen, and say: "This is foolish. You know something of God, I know something of God, why don't we go sit under a tree and talk, and if that does not work, ask a couple of these other fools to help us talk about what God would have us do in this matter?" [*see*: Proverbs 11:14; Matthew 18:15-16; I Corinthians 6:1-6; James 5:13-16.]

Instead [vs. 24]: "So Moses listened to *and* heeded the voice of his father-in-law and did all that he had said."

This does not say that Moses sought wisdom from God.

Thus, in light of my thesis, I think this was not God's choice. I think that in part from my inability as a judge to meet the clear and present "great" needs of those who came before me — and in part because, as part of a team of "listeners who speak truth," I saw miraculous things take place in Matthew 18:16 settings.

The husband and wife in the basement with the three kids was a miracle within our system because a judge chose without thought to step out of the system for a moment.

Paul David Tripp, in *Instruments in the Redeemer's Hands: People in Need of Change Helping People in Need of Change* (P&R Publishing, 2002) said this [@ pg xi]:

What God has ordained for his church is both wonderful and sobering. It is wonderful because he is a jealous and determined God. His work in his people will not fail, but will continue until it is completed. It is sobering because this work follows an "all of my people, all of the time model."

Many of us would be relieved if God had placed our sanctification in the hands of trained and paid professionals, but that simply is not the biblical model. God's plan is that through the faithful ministry of every part, the whole body will grow to full maturity in Christ. The leaders of His church have been gifted, positioned, and appointed to train and mobilize the people of God for this "every person, everyday" ministry lifestyle.

The paradigm is simple: when God calls you to himself, he also calls you to be a servant, an instrument in his redeeming hands. All of his children are called into ministry, and each of them needs the daily intervention this ministry provides. If you follow the Lord for a thousand years, you would still need the ministry of the body of Christ as much as you did the day you first believed. This need will remain until our sanctification is complete in Glory.

This concept does not envision the 78,600 Judges of Jethro, but the ones and twos of Matthew 18:16, I Corinthians 6:1-6, and James 5:13-16.

If there is any *Truth* in all that I have said to this point, then you have to admit that God's giving of the Law was an act of Great Grace.

I told my students that God's Law is like a *plotnik's otbec* (carpenter's plumb line): it allows us to see when we are not "plumb" – when and where we have fallen short of His Glory – and shows us our need for self-correction, in which His Spirit will help us.

For such moments, God *instructs* us rather than *threaten us with punishment* because He wants us to be restored to Him. His *ways* are designed to encourage us to walk them – coming out of the bushes, back to Him, and back to those we have hurt. It is the way of Confession and Forgiveness.

His *way* is why He can promise us:

Therefore, [there is] now no condemnation (no adjudging guilty of wrong [WDB: i.e., of a wrong essential nature]) for those who are in Christ Jesus, *who live [and] walk not after the dictates of the flesh, but after the dictates of the Spirit.*" [Romans 8:1.]

There is a great difference between *conviction* and *condemnation*.

Condemnation paralyzes and leaves one hopeless and helpless.

You see, we <u>do</u> know what we have done, as did Adam, and Eve; we <u>do</u> know whom we have hurt. But we can't see anything we can do to make things right. So we stand frozen in position, fearful to move, lest someone find us out, reject us, or punishes us.

A sense of condemnation is one of the *consequences* of our Criminal Justice system because both the *Purpose* and *Method* for the system are wrong.

Condemnation is a horror, and it is not God's Way.

Conviction, in contrast, precedes sentence.

It is a declaration of the *truth* of the fact that you caused a harm, allowing you to, if you choose, agree with God that you are responsible for your act done, that you recognize a responsibility to acknowledge that fact to those whom you have hurt, and that you have a responsibility to take such steps as are possible at the moment to help right the consequences of the harm done.

Conviction is what God's Spirit is constantly striving to bring into the life of all mankind.

Conviction calls our attention to the wrong we have done, and to those whom we have hurt in the process. It invites us to "agree with God" that what we did was wrong "before Him", i.e., "sin." It asks us to commit to a new path – a path we do not know where it will take us, or where it will end, or what it will look like as we walk, but a path we can walk one step at a time because He is with us, we are *right* with Him, He knows the future, and we no longer need to know the future because we are in His Light and Life; i.e., we walk in faith and not by sight. [See: Romans 8:28, 37-39.]

It is for all of the above reasons that I see Psalms 119 – the *Psalm of the Law* – as a hymn of thanksgiving to a gracious God who knows our need to know how to live, and who gives us (a) His written guidance, (b) the picture of Himself in the Son walking the earth for three years, (c) His indwelling Spirit, and (d) the *ekklesia*, Body of Christ, to assist us in making choices.

I would also refer the reader to the Hebrew word, *derek*, translated as *ways* in passages such as Deuteronomy 32:4 and Psalm 103:7, where God's *ways* are equated with *righteousness*, *law* and *justice*. [*Vine's*, Hebrew, pg 284.]

In contrast to all of this, I don't know of anyone who sings a hymn of praise to our Criminal Code!

In summation, I find nothing to support the idea that God's *law* is punitive in its essential nature, or given for a purpose of deterring conduct.

God created us with free will – the ability to choose – and that freedom can always override any fear of punishment. If you doubt that, go into the prisons and ask those you meet if they knew what they were doing was a crime, and whether they were thinking about getting caught and punished when they did the crime.

And so I close this chapter with a question:

To what extent can God's principles and *ways* be brought into our criminal justice systems so that those brought to the system might be encouraged to walk His *way* without terror?

I am working on a book on that issue, with a working title of "Towards a Biblical View of Criminal Justice," and hope to complete it in 2019.

The Role of the Believer, the Body, and the Organized Church

Does the Body of Christ in the U.S. not practice I Corinthians 6:1-8, James 5:13-16, Matthew 5:20-26 and 18:12-20 because we have been brain washed into believing our secular law system produces *Justice*?

Or do we fear our vision of an angry God more than man?

If a nation of 150,000,000 people (Russia) can exist for 1000- years and handle their own conflicts without our vaunted Rule of Law and Due Process, might we think it worth considering their ways, even if we will not accept Paul's inspired thoughts from I Cor. 6:1-8?

There are two more stories from my life in the old USSR which illustrate another aspect of life under a totalitarian-based system:

I asked Vaghan early on how he and other business men dealt with their business conflicts. I knew they had an arbitration mechanism among merchants, but I wanted to know about other types of business conflicts.

"Well, he said," I get my *krisha*."

"*Krisha*", I said. "what is that"?

"My roof", he replied.

"Makes no sense", I said.

"My *krisha* is someone I know and trust for their wisdom and truth speaking. The one I have a conflict with gets his *krisha*, I get mine, and we all meet and work things out", says Vaghan.

After 2 weeks in Moscow using a bathtub as a clothes washer, we decided to use our meager resources to get a Western washing machine. When we moved to Minsk,

Belarus, I went with Oleg to "comparison shop" for a clothes washer. We found a good buy, and agreed to meet the next day to make the purchase — after I went home and got the cash from the stash.

The next day, I got to the location a few minutes early, saw a line leading to the Government Money Exchange Booth, and promptly got in line. By the time Oleg appeared, the line was longer behind me, but had not moved in front of me. Since I had simply jumped into the line, I didn't even know if the Bank was open (in Minsk they often were not), and asked Oleg to check. He went, looked and came back to report it was open. "But, Oleg", I said, "the line is not moving." So he went forward again, this time having a word with those in front of me. When he reached the front of the line, he beckoned me: "You're next!" Strange, but I went forward, slid six, $100 bills through the slot (with two people peering over my shoulders), got a bag full of Belarusian Rubles, and walked 20-feet to buy the machine where the money was counted by another person who saw me get it.

As I walked, I saw out of the corner of my eye a strange thing take place: from the back of the waiting line, people began passing Belarusian money forward to the front of the line (there were about a dozen people in the line by then). The person at the front of the line slid the collective gatherings in through the slot, got some U.S. dollars, and the crowd collectively walked away. "Oleg", I said, "*stoi eta?*" ["What gives?"]

The Belarusian currency is not a "hard currency". From September 1995 when we arrived, to June 1999 when we left, the exchange rate went from 1,100 Belarusian Rubles to the dollar to 300,000 — 600,000 if you exchanged on the street, which was illegal — or 1.2 million if you wanted to use it to import goods from abroad into Belarus. Thus it was necessary for every person, in order to survive, to exchange excess Rubles for Dollars.

Each Belarusian is a member of at least one "collective" – about fifteen people, trusted implicitly. Every day, one member of the collective is appointed to spend the day "in line" doing things for all. Thus, each person in that line looking for dollars "held the stake" of at least fourteen others, whose lives depended on finding dollars. But as to one another, everybody in that line was a stranger, and normally not to be trusted.

Yet, knowing the common need they instinctively and immediately formed a new collective when they saw my $600. When they adjourned, it was to find a place where the one with the dollars could find out what each one had "put into the pot", and arrange a method of breaking the dollars into smaller amounts for distribution – a process done with absolute honesty.

"This," said Oleg proudly, "is how we survive."

God's Methods Expanded

If you have stuck with me to this point, then you must realize that <u>if</u> God's *Purpose* for law is not to try to deter evil through determining the condition of the mind, and not to punish people but rather give teachings so we might know how to live truly free, and to give His people a path to follow to come back to God when we sin, <u>then</u> God's *Method* must be a process to offer the opportunity for His *Purpose* to be fulfilled.

Well, let me declare as a praise of Him and His *Ways*, that He has given us a gracious method. So, let's look at it.

Step #1: <u>Overlooking a transgression</u>:

> **Proverbs 17:9**: He who covers *and* forgives an offense seeks love, but he who repeats *or* harps on a matter separates even close friends.

Do you acknowledge that you, at times, do dumb and stupid things which hurt others? Would you hope that they might overlook your stupid thing and remain in good relationship with you, as opposed to spreading tales about your errors to others? If so, won't you do the same for them when they hurt you without malice?

> **Proverbs 17:14**: The beginning of strife is as when water first trickles [from a crack in a dam]; therefore stop contention before it becomes worse *and* quarreling breaks out.

Step #2: <u>Reprove in love</u>: But, you say: "He keeps on doing it to me!"

Proverbs 17:10: A reproof enters deeper into a man of understanding than a hundred lashes into a [self-confident] fool.

Ephesians 4:15: Rather, let our lives lovingly express truth [in all things, speaking truth, dealing truly, living truly].

Step #3: <u>Seeking Counsel</u>: "I have tried, but nothing is working."

Proverbs 11:14: Where no wise guidance is, the people fall, but in the multitude of counselors there is safety.

James 5:13-16: Is anyone among you afflicted (ill-treated, suffering evil)? He should pray. Is anyone glad at heart? He should sing praise to God. Is anyone among you sick? He should call in the church elders (the spiritual guides). And they should pray over him, anointing him with oil in the Lord's name. And the prayer [that is] of faith will save him who is sick, and the Lord will restore him; and if he has committed sins, he will be forgiven. Confess to one another therefore your faults (your slips, your false steps, your offenses, your sins) and pray [also] for one another that you may be healed *and* restored [to a spiritual tone of mind and heart]. The earnest (heartfelt, continued) prayer of a righteous man makes tremendous power available [dynamic in its working].

I Corinthians 6:1-3: Does any of your dare, when he has a matter of complaint against another [*heteros*: generic person], to go to law before unrighteous men [men neither upright nor right with God, laying it before them] instead of before the saints (the people of God)? Do you not know that the saints (the believers) will [one day] judge *and* govern the world? And if the world [itself] is to be judges *and* ruled by you, are you unworthy *and* incompetent to try [such petty matters] of the smallest courts of justice? Do you not know also that we [Christians] are to judge the [very] angels *and* pronounce opinion between right and wrong [for them]? How much more then [as to] matters pertaining to this world *and* of this life only!

These passages, while addressing different situations, work together. The common theme is: You have a problem and know not what to do, so get together with a couple of Believers, lay it before them, and search the Scriptures and pray together, seeking God's wisdom and direction.

I suggest you begin by asking God who He has placed in your life at this very time as a *helper* to you. But be sure to have at least two others, and to do this face-to-face; phoning different people and telling them a story has a danger of changing the story while you seek agreement with what you have already decided you want to do. A team helps you avoid double-mindedness, and find God's *way*.

I Corinthians 6:3-5 is actually written for a commercial conflict, and an arbitrated decision by the brethren when the matter involves two brethren [*adelphos*, "of the same womb" (Verse 6), which replaces *heteros* (in Verse 1, "the other person"). Thus verse 1 is unlimited and, in my opinion, reinforces the two prior references.

Step #4: <u>Go and seek out the other party to talk about things</u>:

> **Matthew 5:21-26**: You have heard that it was said to the men of old, You shall not kill, and whoever kills shall be liable to *and* unable to escape the <u>punishment</u> imposed by the court; and whoever speaks contemptuously *and* insultingly to his <u>brother</u> shall be shall be liable to *and* unable to escape the <u>punishment</u> imposed by the Sanhedrin, and whoever says, You cursed fool! [You empty-headed idiot]! shall be liable to *and* unable to escape the hell (Gehenna) of fire. So if when you are offering your gift at the altar you there remember that your brother has any [grievance] against you, leave your gift at the altar, and go. First make peace with your brother, and then come back

and present your gift. Come to terms quickly with your accuser while you are on the way traveling with him, lest your accuser hand you over to the judge, and the judge to the guard, and you be put in prison. Truly I say to you, you will not be released until you have paid the last fraction of a penny.

Please note that the references to *punishment* in the quote are all things "You have heard it said"; i.e., their culture is saying this is the way of things. Jesus then turns from the world's sense of things to God's view of the tongue as an expression of the inner person – and then launches into a teaching on the importance of our seeking resolution of conflict even when we believe we have done nothing wrong! His ways really are so very different than ours."

At the heart of God, His instructions are given because He desires resolution of conflict, and reconciliation with Him and with others more than a sacrifice, church attendance, or singing hymns [*see*: Amos 5:21-24.]

Matthew 18:10-20: Beware that you do not despise *or* feel scornful toward *or* think little of one of these little ones, for I tell you that in heaven their angels always are in the presence off *and* look upon the face of My Father Who is in heaven. *For the Son of man came to save (from the penalty of eternal death] that which was lost.*

What do you think? If a man has a hundred sheep, and one of them has gone astray *and* gets lost, will he not leave the ninety-nine on the mountain and go in search of the one that is lost? And if it should be that he finds it, truly I say to you, he rejoices more over it than over the ninety-nine that did not get lost. Just so it is not the will of My Father Who is in heaven that one of these little ones should be lost *and* perish.

If your brother wrongs you, go and show him his fault between you and him privately. If he listens to you, you have won back your brother. But if he does not hear, take along with you one or two others, so that every word

[Greek: *rhema*] may be confirmed [Greek: *histemi*] *and* upheld by the testimony of two or three witnesses. If he pays no attention to them [refusing to listen and obey], tell it to the church [Greek: *ekklesia*]; and if he refuses to listen even to the church, let him be to you as a pagan and a tax collector.

Truly I say to you, whatever you forbid *and* declare to be improper and unlawful on earth must be what is already forbidden in heaven, and whatever you permit *and* declare proper and lawful on earth must be what is already permitted in heaven. Truly I tell you, if two of you on earth agree (harmonize together, make a symphony together) about whatever [anything and everything] they may ask, it will come to pass *and* be done for them by My Father in heaven. For wherever two or three are gathered (drawn together as My followers) in (into) My name, there I AM in the midst of them.

Both Matthew 5:21-26 and 18:10-20 refer to conflicts between *brothers*, the Greek word for which is *adelfos*, and signifies *of the same womb*. To a Christian, this means a fellow Christian.

In I Cor. 6:1, Paul refers to conflicts with *heteros*, "another of a different kind", i.e., even a non-believer, but switches to *adelfos* in verse 6.

I show these distinctions because I want to encourage readers to think that the *principles* in these three passages can be used as guidelines for any conflict, with any person, at any time. You might not have another church to help out, but there may be mutually trusted friends, business organizations, etc which could help speak *Truth* to the deaf and blind.

As but one example, my Christian dentist in Minneapolis had a pamphlet on the table in the waiting room which invited his patients to submit any conflict with him to a *peer review* panel of dentist. The dentist was bound by the decisions of his/her peers, but not the patient. He told me that over 95% of all claims of the participating dentists were resolved this way.

We live in a fallen world among fallen people, yet God proves that His instruction work in even that situation if we will but practice them.

The above 4-steps present a number of principles:

A. God wants people who have complaints against one another to first talk to one another, regardless of whether a person thinks they are a *victim* or are being called an *offender*. From God's perspective, the talking is of greater importance than engaging in religious activity.

B. If talking to one another will not get the job done, get some other people involved, up to and including the entire organization you or the other party might be a part of [Matthew 18:17]. The purpose is *conversation* in hope that *Truth* might be spoken and accepted, and confession and forgiveness loosed so reconciliation of relationship, and resolution of the conflict, might take place.

C. Don't gossip to others before going to the one with whom you have a problem. [Really learn to not gossip or receive gossip under any circumstances!]

D. When you go, prepare yourself, possibly with the help of counselors, to confess and forgive as appropriate. One of the best tools I know for preparing yourself to go to the other is *The Peacemaker* (Baker Books, 1991), by my friend, Ken Sande.

E. When you decide that you need to "take one or two" with you, think first and foremost in terms of: "Who might the other listen to?" Often that will mean taking *their* friends, not *your* friends. This is as it should be, for you are not engaged in trying to win a case in court, but to win another back to righteous actions.

F. In selecting people, you are not necessarily looking for a court-room witness of a past event, and certainly not people to serve as *judges*. You are looking for someone to, as the Greek text shows best: "boldly stand upright [*histemi*], God's very Word [*rhema*] for the Moment" —

> *histemi* (2476), (a) transitively, denotes "to cause to stand, to set"; in passive voice, "to be made to stand" …[*Vine's* Greek pg 598.]

rhema – ... "the sword of the Spirit, which is the word of God," Ephesians 6:17; here the reference is not to the whole Bible as such, but to the individual scriptures which the Spirit brings to our remembrance for use in time of need, a prerequisite being the regular storing of the mind with Scripture. [*Vine's*, Greek, pg 683.]

G. This process is designed to start with no rules, regulations, or procedures, and no preconceived outcomes. It is a *conversation*, with the help of others, not knowing where it will end, but entered into to honor God who gave the *Instruction* to come and talk. It is an act of faith to participate. When others are brought in to help, they come not as mediators or arbitrators at law, nor are they merely facilitators, for they come with a bias – to serve God and speak His *Word* for the moment.

H. These people may judge words and actions/inactions against God's standards, but they do not judge *character* or *outcomes*. They don't give *awards* or *order behavior*; they don't arbitrate or adjudicate an outcome. Rather they remind the parties of sin, the need for confession and forgiveness, and the need to *do justice* as they are moved by God during the process and/or afterwards. This is not the Old Testament trial of Deuteronomy 19:15 – where court-room eye witnesses are involved.

One witness shall not prevail against a man for any crime or any wrong in connection with any sin he commits; only on the testimony of two or three witnesses shall a charge be established.

You see, when you are in conflict, you have only a few possible outcomes:

(a) be reconciled;
(b) confess, forgive, and *do justice* from your side regardless of what the other does, so that you may receive God's *Justice* (peace within) rather than allow the pain of the offense to become a "root of resentment (rancor, bitterness, or hatred) [which] shoots

forth and causes trouble *and* bitter torment, and many become contaminated *and* defiled by it." [Hebrews 12:15.]; or

(c) go to war and risk having all of those negative things.

The whole idea of restoring and reconciling can also be seen in the Matthew 18:12-14 passage if we recognize that we are talking about a *sheep* — not a cute little *lamb* wrapped around the neck of the Good Shepherd as sometimes portrayed on T-shirts.

This is a *stray sheep* who may have picked up a lot of trash and waste while roaming wild. For a marvelous example of the type of *stray sheep* Jesus is thinking of, see *Chris, the Australian Sheep*: *http://www.bbc.com/news/world-australia-34135805.*

You will love it!

The Victim Offender Reconciliation program in Elkhart County, which we started in 1978, was merely a secularized version of the Matthew 18 passage – but God still worked within it.

The story of my difficulties as Judge, set forth in Colson's *Loving God*, focused on an offender who went through the VORP process one-by- one with his 12 victims. One victim (from whom he had stolen all the wedding gifts while they were on their Honeymoon), bought the offender, his wife and child coats the first winter he was out of prison, because they were in need. When the offender was sent back to prison for my error of law, two victims alternated going to see him in prison each week – the one who bought the coats, and a deputy sheriff whose home he had also broken into.

Yes, even in what we see as very serious criminal acts (he broke into, as I recall, 12 homes when the owners were out), victims and offenders can find peace with one another – God's "peace which passes all understanding". It is that peace which has become, to me, the only definition I know for *Justice*.

You might remember that I told you that today, in Kazakhstan, they, having heard some of these principles, allow mediation of criminal cases when the parties are willing.

Another thing found in the *Torah* are references to *restitution*, with multiple amounts, and with a portion for the Temple.

In Romans 13:8, our instruction is to "owe nothing but love".

One thing which takes place in a Matthew 18 (and often in VORP proceedings), was "an outcome", the nature of which might never have been envisioned by anyone except God. But because He knows the hearts of all those involved in the process (which includes the witnesses), He knows that which will bring the greatest healing to one or more.

> In a I Corinthians 6 arbitration between two Christian businessmen, the Lord helped the panel come to a conclusion of who should pay what to whom – and then we suddenly and spontaneously added that it should be done monthly by delivering a portion of the debt by check to the door of the one "due it."

> It turned out that God knew the two men had "played a game with the process" while never wanting to see the face of the other again; we did not catch that.

> After six months of delivering a check to the door, the Spirit broke through these two hard hearts and they cried on the shoulders of one another over their foolishness.

> In another I Corinthians 6 arbitration, the employer was moved by God to forgive (cancel forever) a $20,000 debt of a prior employee, and rehire the employee at an increase of wage to compensate for what he had lost in income from being fired. The employer did so in joy, having been convicted by God of his shortcomings with his wife and in his business transactions. Many thought the employer had been taken advantage of.

> Two years later, the employer made a loan to another person, and lost the money. For the employer's wife, it was the last straw, and she filed for divorce. The previously forgiven employee spent six-months walking back and forth between them until their marriage was restored.

> God's restitution in God's way at God's time?!

To show that God's processes can be used by our modern systems, I refer you again to *R. v. Moses* and *The New Zealand Experiment*.

When Ellen and I were in Fiji to minister reconciliation among the people, our host received a strange invitation: the Professional Mediators of Fiji (paid by the State and used pre-trial in matters involving labor vs. management disputes), wanted to know what the difference was between what they did in their "cases" from what we do in our "cases", and the reasons for the differences.

We spent an hour breaking down the matter of using teams of peace-presenters and being "biased witnesses to *Truth*". They then spent another hour in conversation with their director about "if and how" they could adopt our mechanisms into their system.

And so I want you to know some of the essences of the team approach:

1. Our *methods* are nor *Professional Counseling.* Professional Counseling is nearly always a trained professional counseling a lay person, one-on-one. The danger is that: (a) the client may not be able to "hear" the professional for some reasons; (b) the professional may have personal issues which impede their ability to give wise, full, and accurate counsel; (c) the professional has been taught to not share of their own personal struggles and experiences, while God seems to think such sharing is important for encouragement of the counselee [*see,* II Corinthians 1:3-5]; and, (d) Peace-presenters can get personally involved in the lives of those needing peace, but professional counselors can't do that.

   Therefore, we use teams of "counselors". The Bible says: "where no wise guidance is, the people fall; but in the multitude of counselors there is safety." [Proverbs 11:14; see also James 5:13-16, wherein *rhema*, God's living and active *word*, might be substituted for *oil*.] It also allows the counselors to come into unity, and that display of unity has its own power to help people in conflict come into unity. It also avoids double mindedness in the client in that the counselors all hear the same story at the same time, which makes giving of unified counsel easier and more likely.

2. We also use lay people in the vast majority of situations, with minimal training, but hearts desiring to honor God, and bring in a professional, as needed, to be an advisor to the "counselors".

3. Each party is allowed to bring one or two helpers with them. The "counselors" then merge these helpers into the team. This is helpful because a person in conflict may never hear anyone except a trusted friend and, after all, we are only trying to get people to listen and "hear", to "take deep within their self and appropriate" that which is being said.

4. We also allow counselors and helpers to get personally involved with the "clients" because:

> II Corinthians 1:3-5: Blessed be the God and Father of our Lord Jesus Christ, the Father of sympathy (pity and mercy) and the God [Who is the Source] of every comfort, Who comforts (consoles and encourages) us in every trouble (calamity and affliction) so that we may also be able to comfort (console and encourage) those who are in any kind of trouble or distress, with the comfort (consolation and encouragement) with which we ourselves are comforted (consoled and encouraged) by God. For just as Christ's [own] sufferings fall to our lot [as they overflow upon His disciples, and we share and experience them] abundantly, so through Christ comfort (consolation and encouragement) is also [shared and experienced] freely by us.

Is this transparence risky? To the counselor, yes, for they become vulnerable and open. But to the clients? No; they can only gain in such a process.

5. By using multiple counselors, the counselors can give more time to each client and, as necessary, meet practical burdens of the conflict that a professional can't consider doing.

6. By using lay counselors (likely volunteers), the service can be free. Why should one who believes they are righteous be further victimized by having to pay for help? I was impressed that the government of Fiji paid their mediators as encouragement for the people to see the program as something the State desired for the benefit of all the people.

103

7. A professional counselor must always be "neutral". A Biblical peacemaker is neutral as between the parties, and neutral as to any outcome, but they are not neutral as to God and His *Truth*. While the world seems to have given up on *Truth*, and made it politically incorrect to speak *Truth*, *Truth* is at the heart of *Philip, New Zealand,* and *Matt. 18:16* – so the real issue is not the speaking of it, but its Source and how it is spoken, i.e.:

   a) It must be spoken "without condemnation" so that it may bring "conviction".
   b) It is spoken without demand, hoping one will hear *truth*, accept it as such, and act this transformation out in the future – bringing forth fruit in its own season and manner.

8. In normal counseling, mediation and arbitration activities the professional works to bring people to an <u>agreement</u>. Christian conciliation does not seek an agreement as much as it does getting *Truth* to be heard as *Truth*. When that is successful, we trust the parties will act justly towards one another, under the guidance of God's Spirit.

9. Lastly, in the Christian conciliation process we are not time sensitive; time and boxes of Kleenex are major resources us!

Finally, please go to *www.shepherdsforpeace.com* and look for the *Flow Chart* on Matthew 18:12-20 which shows how sin-within leads to an outward act, which then calls forth loving *Truth- speaking*, hopefully opening the door for the Spirit to bring conviction and a repentant heart.

Following the appearance of the repentant heart and restoration to fellowship, counseling can help one possibly see their sin-within – the things which control his emotions and behavior – and allow for assisting one-another in change of behaviors.

In all of this, a revival is waiting to break forth as the congregation hears and sees one who has been transformed by God. There are many instances where a testimony of reconciliation between people launched revivals which swept the nation. [See Google: Canadian Revival of 1971, and Asbury College Revival, as examples.]

Conclusion

And so, I close by re-stating my questions:

When you are conflicted, does your image of God send you into the bushes in fear, or allow you to overcome your inner self screaming at you, and come out of the bushes?

Will you seek out your fellow Believers when in need of counsel, instead of seeking after the ways of man?

Are you willing to allow your past failures to be poured out by God to help another gain strength to confess and forgive in their conflict?

In all of this, please remember this:

> No conflict is ever too late, nor too big, nor too complex for one to find peace within it when they walk out God's ways:
>
>> We are assured *and* know that [God being a partner in their labor] all things work together *and* are [fitting into a plan] for good to *and* for those who love God and are called according to [His] design *and* purpose. [Romans 8:28.]

And so I return to the second part of Paul's Brief at Romans 12:1-21:

> Verses 1-3: the necessary things which every believer must work on: <u>dedicate</u> your body (and self) to God, <u>break off</u> conformance with the things of the world, <u>transform</u> your mind, ideals and attitude with the things of God, and don't think more highly of your efforts that you should, but evaluate yourself by your known failures.
>
> Verses 4-5: a declaration of the existence of a new thing called the Body of Christ, where you may interact in safety because of love.

Verses 6-13: recognition of the uniqueness of each member of the Body, the love that binds them together, the need to work on living in harmony, and the gifts they bring to the table in peace-presenting.

Verses 14-20: instructions for living in the world as opposed to within the Body.

Finally, as to the Image of God and His ways, consider this:

I John 2:3-6: And this is how we may discern [daily by experience] that we are coming to know Him [to perceive, recognize, understand and become better acquainted with Him]: if we keep (bear in mind, observe, practice) His teachings (precepts, commandments). Whoever says, "I know Him [I perceived, recognize, understand and am acquainted with Him] but fails to keep *and* obey His commandments (teachings) is a liar, and the Truth [of the Gospel] is not in him. But he who keeps (treasures) His Word [who bears in mind His precepts, who observes His message in its entirety], truly in him has the love of *and* for God been perfected (completed, reached maturity). By this we may perceive (know, recognize and be sure) that we are in Him: Whoever says he abides in Him ought [as a personal debt] to walk *and* conduct himself in the same way in which He walked *and* conducted Himself.

In all that I have written, you should sense that I see the role of the Body of Christ as being deeply involved in counseling one-another into life-for-the-moment when in a conflict with self, God, and/or others.

And so I return to the Garden of Eden, and close with words of Jay Adams from *A Theology of Christian Counseling* (Zondervan 1979, pg 1):

From the beginning, human change depended upon counseling. Man was created as a being whose very existence is derived from and dependent upon a Creator whom he must acknowledge as such and from whom he must obtain wisdom and knowledge through revelation.

The purpose and meaning of his life, as well as his very existence, is derived and dependent. He can find none of this in himself. Man is not autonomous.

"In the beginning was the Word" (John 1:1) says it all. Man needed God's Word from the onset — *even before the fall*. His revelatory Word was necessary to understand God, creation, himself, his proper relationships to others, his place and functions in creation, and his limitations.

May God bless you and keep you, strengthen and guide you, for His Glory through Christ Jesus. Amen.

William "Bill" Bontrager, J.D.

Postscript

On October 27th, 2018, I spoke to two groups of inmates at two chapel services inside a maximum security prison. To each, I began with two questions:

> "Is your image of God that of an angry judge pointing at you with outstretched arm and a bony figure?"

> "Do you think the Bible is God's law-code for crime and punishment?"

In each instance, for each question, every hand went up.
And so I asked another question:

> "Will you listen to me as I try to tell you why your images are wrong?"

No hand went up.

While I pray my words about the image of a Good God and His gracious instructions will move some to take steps to find peace and justice behind the walls, their reaction also raised two questions for me to ponder:

> "What does this say about the nature of our Criminal and Juvenile justice systems, and the need to radically transform them?"

> "To what extent would any given congregation answer the first two questions in the same way, and what lessons might a church draw from such a congregational response?"

I am taking the first of these into consideration as I work on *Towards A Biblical View of "Criminal" "Justice"*.

Scripture References

Printed in the United States
By Bookmasters